Food for America's Future

FOOD
for America's Future

*Twelve Outstanding Authorities Discuss
the Country's Ability to Feed
Its Multiplying Millions*

BOOKS FOR LIBRARIES PRESS
PLAINVIEW, NEW YORK

Library of Congress Cataloging in Publication Data

Ethyl Corporation.
    Food for America's future.
    (Essay index reprint series)
    1. Agriculture--United States.   2. Food supply--
United States.   I. Title.
[S441.E78 1973]   338.1'9'73   72-14156
ISBN 0-518-10009-X

In dedicating this book to the memory of
CHARLES F. KETTERING
scientist, inventor, and philanthropist,
Ethyl Corporation, of which he was a founder,
first president, and senior director,
pays tribute to his broad range of interests and studies,
which included the phenomenon of photosynthesis

Foreword

THROUGHOUT the years, the plentiful supplies of foods and fibers of this country's farms have fed and clothed an ever-increasing population at home and have helped meet the needs of many peoples abroad.

But there is real concern in many quarters that this era of abundance may, in the not too distant future, be replaced by one of enforced abstinence. More and more, people are raising questions about America's ability, in the years to come, to feed just her own people, to say nothing of those in other parts of the world. Today, for the first time since the early colonists scratched out their bare existence from the soil, serious doubts are being expressed about this country's food potential.

The world-wide population explosion that has been going on since World War II is cause for concern. At present rates, 50 million people a year are being added to the earth's inhabitants, and the United States is in no sense exempt from this. In the foreseeable future of 1975—just 15 years hence—there will be 65 million more mouths to feed than there are today, or a total of 245 million. This is equivalent to adding as many people as now live in the 22 continental states west of the Mississippi River, plus those in Indiana. This poses a multi-million-mouth problem. Every individual, every industry and government agency, and every social, political, and economic group is involved.

There is no simple solution to the problem; there are no pat answers. But a clear view of the problem and of the prospects for solving it can be important and helpful. With this in mind Ethyl Corporation went to men who are well informed in research, soil science, education, farm machinery and power, agricultural chemicals, food processing and marketing, and economics. We asked these men to outline briefly what has been done, what is being done, and what can and probably will be done to better equip the farms and industries of America to provide ample food for America's future. This book is the result.

Starting with the basic question of America's land capability and progressing through other essential fields, these authorities tell of the tremendous strides that have been made in food production, processing, and distribution. They report on what's going on "down on the farm" right now. And finally, they draw aside the curtain and look ahead over the next decade and a half.

Will America be able to feed its 245 million people in 1975? The opinion of these men is a unanimous "yes." Their views on how and how well America will be fed 15 years from now and further on into the future are interesting, informative, and reassuring, and are presented here as a public service.

B. B. TURNER
President, Ethyl Corporation

Contents

Foreword   vii

How Many People Can We Feed?   3
  Firman E. Bear
  EDITOR-IN-CHIEF, *Soil Science*

Research for Abundance   17
  Byron T. Shaw
  ADMINISTRATOR, AGRICULTURAL RESEARCH SERVICE
  UNITED STATES DEPARTMENT OF AGRICULTURE

Miracle of the Green Plant   31
  Thomas A. Boyd
  CONSULTANT, GENERAL MOTORS RESEARCH STAFF

New Horizons in Education   43
  Clifford M. Hardin
  CHANCELLOR, UNIVERSITY OF NEBRASKA

Management of Land, Labor and Capital   57
  Herrell F. DeGraff
  BABCOCK PROFESSOR OF FOOD ECONOMICS
  CORNELL UNIVERSITY

Insect, Disease and Weed Control   67
  Richard C. McCurdy
  PRESIDENT, SHELL CHEMICAL COMPANY

Making Land More Productive   83
  Kenneth S. Adams
  CHAIRMAN OF THE BOARD, PHILLIPS PETROLEUM COMPANY

Increasing Productivity by Power Farming   99
  Robert S. Stevenson
  PRESIDENT, ALLIS-CHALMERS MANUFACTURING COMPANY

Energy in Abundance   109
  Robert E. Wilson
  CHAIRMAN OF THE BOARD (RETIRED)
  STANDARD OIL COMPANY OF INDIANA

Electricity and the Business of Farming   123
  Philip D. Reed
  CHAIRMAN OF THE BOARD (RETIRED)
  GENERAL ELECTRIC COMPANY

More and Better Food for More People   137
  Charles G. Mortimer
  CHAIRMAN AND CHIEF EXECUTIVE
  GENERAL FOODS CORPORATION

The Man on the Farm   153
  Charles B. Shuman
  PRESIDENT, AMERICAN FARM BUREAU FEDERATION

Food for America's Future

Firman E. Bear, editor-in-chief of Soil Science, *research scientist, and writer, has served in both industrial and educational circles. From 1940 to 1954, he was professor of agricultural chemistry and chairman of the soils department at Rutgers University. Dr. Bear has been active in many scientific societies, and is a past president of the American Society of Agronomy, the Soil Science Society of America and the Soil Conservation Society of America.*

How Many People Can We Feed?

Firman E. Bear

ONE of the remarkable facts about the 48 states that constitute the mainland of the United States of America is the very large area encompassed within their boundaries. These states contain 1,904 million acres of land and an additional 29 million acres of water. Only the U.S.S.R., China, Canada, and Brazil encompass greater areas.

All the states on the mainland lie within the warmer

portion of the North Temperate Zone. No one of them
is subject to such continuously torrid temperatures and
torrential rains as are experienced in the tropics. Nor
does any one of them have the frigid temperatures and
long-lasting winters of the Arctic regions. Our moder-
ate but quickly changeable and highly stimulating
climate is responsible in large part for the exceptional
vitality of our people.

The mainland is also favored with very large reserves
of ore, petroleum, gas, oil shale, and coal, vast areas
of excellent cropland, and an estimated 13 billion tons
of phosphate rock, a priceless asset to our agriculture.
Because of these climatic and economic advantages,
the rate of development of the 48 states during the more
than three and a half centuries since the first perma-
nent English settlement was established at Jamestown,
Virginia, has been very rapid. And the agricultural
and industrial future of the United States looks very
promising.

The land area of the mainland will remain essentially
as it is now. But this characteristic does not apply to
the people who inhabit it, and there is no dependable
evidence that it ever will. The population of the United
States is rapidly increasing and, as a consequence, the
land area per person is steadily declining. Each of the

800,000 Indians who originally inhabited the mainland had 2,400 acres of land at his disposal. But, as Benjamin Franklin predicted over 200 years ago, the population doubled every 25 years during the early period of the nation's history. It is still growing at a rate of 1.7 per cent a year. For each of our present 180 million people there are only 11 acres; by 1975 the area per person will not exceed 9 acres; and by the year 2000 it will probably have been reduced to less than 6 acres.

Even so, there would still be plenty of land area per person if all of it were good cropland and if its use for the production of food represented our only need for it. Unfortunately, more than half our land is not suitable for growing harvested crops. This is partly because of the mountainous nature of some of it, but lack of adequate rainfall in other large areas is a far more troublesome factor. Some 150 million acres of the mainland are desert, with less than 10 inches of rainfall per year; nearly 600 million acres are semiarid, with a rainfall of only 10 to 20 inches. The climate of over 300 million acres is subhumid; although rainfall in this area averages 20 to 25 inches, periods of drought, often of several years duration, occur from time to time. The greatest hope for this subhumid region lies in wider use of better systems of grassland management by which both water and soil are conserved. Although a dependable yearly rainfall of 25 inches is quite adequate for abundant crop production in the agricultural areas of western Europe, on the western plains of this country it is far from sufficient. The hot, dry, westerly winds that blow over these plains greatly speed up water loss by evaporation from the soil and by transpiration from the leaves of plants.

The 100th meridian, extending southward through the central part of the Dakotas and Nebraska and somewhat west of central Kansas, Oklahoma, and Texas, can be considered the dividing line between the dryland-grazing region to the west and the more moist crop-growing region to the east. Grain farming west of this line is a precarious undertaking, particularly toward the south; though yields in this region may be very high during abnormally wet years, they are distressingly low in dry years.

Some 350 million acres of land are now being devoted to the production of harvested crops. Most of this crop area is in the moist region east of the dividing line; but it includes also some 27 million acres of irrigated arid and semiarid land west of it and a considerable section of the humid region along the West Coast between the Cascade Mountains and the Pacific Ocean.

Additional large acreages of cropland are temporarily in fallow, cover crops, or pasture grasses, or they are lying idle. The total available cropland is now estimated at about 465 million acres. If the need were to arise, and the cost could be justified, we could probably add to this estimated figure some 65 million acres of plowable pasture, 17 million acres of irrigable arid land, 40 million acres of drainable wetlands, and 100 million acres of woodland and forest.

Looking still farther into the future, there are large acreages of salty marshland along our coasts that can be put to agricultural use by diking, pumping, and treating the soil with gypsum. Additional land may also someday be reclaimed, as the Dutch have done, from the seas along our shores. Taking all these possibilities into consideration, it seems reasonable to believe that some 700 million acres of potentially well-watered land on the mainland could ultimately be brought into crop production.

The land resources of Alaska, the forty-ninth state, constitute an additional 365 million acres. With a population of 225,000 the size of the land area per person is almost identical with that enjoyed originally by the Indians on the mainland. But the evidence indicates that Alaska has greater value for strategic purposes for its timber, oil, and mineral resources, and for recreational uses than for its agriculture. With industrial exploitation it may become, on balance, a food-importing state.

Hawaii, the fiftieth state, has a land area of only 4 million acres. With a population already exceeding a half million, its agricultural contribution to the other peoples of the United States will be relatively small in comparison with that of the mainland.

On the mainland good agricultural land is being lost to factories, cities, suburban developments, highways, and recreational areas at the rate of over 1 million acres a year. And the wind and water that are permitted to erode large areas of presently and potentially useful cropland are causing great damage, often beyond the point of repair. These losses of agricultural land are receiving the attention of conservation agencies, of which the largest is the Soil Conservation Service and the conservation districts allied with it. In some localities zoning commissions are now actively engaged in preventing further use of good agricultural land for nonagricultural purposes.

On the other hand, industrial development has also been responsible for the restoration of large acreages of first-class farming land to food production. When tractors and automobiles replaced over 20 million horses and mules, it was no longer necessary to devote large acreages to the growing of the grain and hay that were used to feed these animals. And when the cotton used in the manufacture of clothing and for many other purposes was extensively replaced by synthetic fibers, still more land became available for food production. Large-scale production of air-nitrogen fertilizers also released more land on which food could be grown, it being no longer necessary to grow such extensive acreages of legumes as formerly to collect nitrogen from the air. Other technological advances will undoubtedly be instrumental in making still more land available for food production.

Ways and means designed specifically to increase the area of agricultural land are also being developed. Soil-moving equipment is being used on an ever-larger scale to level land, fill in gullies, and improve the contour. Mesquite, other shrubs, and browse are being uprooted from the soil by huge crawler-type tractors with heavy blades that, in one operation, open up the land to a depth of a foot or more and drop improved grass seed over the turned-up soil. These machines have the capacity to clear and seed brush-ridden land at the rate of 2 to 3 acres per hour per tractor.

Some scientists believe it is possible, and quite dependably so, to make it rain when and where more rain is needed. Experiments in seeding clouds with silver iodide, dry ice, and carbon black have demonstrated important rain-making potentialities. In the Western mountain ranges considerably more rain could be made to fall and thus augment the present supply of water available for irrigation purposes. In arid regions the primary problem is that of finding the right kind of clouds.

Improved procedures have been developed for conserving more of the water that falls as rain in the humid regions. A great variety of new techniques are now being employed to make more of this water soak into the soil instead of allowing it to run off the land surface, often resulting in serious erosion. Most of these conservation measures revolve around contour farming, more frequent growing of sod crops, and improved use of crop wastes by which the surface of the soil is protected against the direct destructive action of wind and rain. The incorporation of crop wastes into the soil also improves the water-absorbing capacity of the soil.

At best, a large part of the rain is carried out to sea

without having served any very useful purpose. Much is now being done to store some of this waste water upstream for supplemental irrigation and industrial use and as an aid to downstream flood control. Some 3 million acres of land in the humid regions are now being irrigated supplementally with water from nearby streams, storage reservoirs, or underground reserves, and a rapid spread of such practices is taking place. And cloud seeding can, conceivably, be practiced to greater advantage in the humid regions of the East than in the drier regions of the West.

Chemical engineers look longingly at the ocean as a possible source of pure water to supplement that falling as rain. New methods for large-scale separation of this pure water from its salts are being sought. Present techniques include distillation, membrane methods, freezing, and use of solvents that separate salt and water. The Department of the Interior reported recently that water can now be obtained from the sea at an estimated cost of about 60 cents per 1,000 gallons. This cost is not too high for water for drinking purposes or even for general household use, and many industries would find it quite acceptable. But it would be entirely too high for cropland-irrigation purposes. The value of the agricultural produce of 1,000 gallons of irrigation water in arid regions is estimated at 10 to 12 cents.

Cost estimates for water from the ocean do not include the cost of raising the water up to the level of the cropland and pushing it into the interior. Although it will probably be a long time before any very large acreages of our arid and semiarid land will be supplied with irrigation water from the Pacific Ocean, it is nevertheless a possibility that does exist. Just how fast this new source of water will be developed will depend primarily on the cost of the energy necessary to purify the water and pipe it to the points where it is needed. At present the potentialities for increasing agricultural production in the areas of adequate rainfall are so high in relation to our needs that we are not too concerned with such problems as these. If by the year 2000 we have a greater need to extract water from clouds and seas, we should, by that time, have a much better understanding of how to proceed.

But little can be done with most of our range and nonplowable pasture lands except to improve their grass cover and make the best possible use of this forage by grazing it with cattle and sheep. The most dependable means of increasing acre yields on land now being farmed and on land still available for farming in the humid regions is by the use of larger quantities of soil amendments in the growing of ever-better-bred plants. These soil amendments include liming materials for correcting the acidity of rain-leached soils, gypsum for overcoming the undue alkalinity and salinity of irrigated arid land, and nitrogen and mineral fertilizers for increasing acre yields the country over. Well over 40 million tons of such chemicals are now being used yearly in this country, and as the need arises, these tonnages can readily be stepped up to much higher levels.

Some 500,000 tons of other chemicals, including the various pesticides now being used mostly for the control of insects, diseases, and weeds on the more intensive crops, are employed annually for crop-protection purposes. And the use of pesticides is being rapidly expanded to include protection of grains, legumes, and grasses. Additional biological controls, such as laboratory-bred parasites, are also being employed on an ever-larger scale. A great deal of work is being done also in the breeding of insect- and disease-resistant strains of plants and in stimulating more rapid growth of plants and greater productiveness of livestock by the use of factory-produced hormonal and antibiotic substances.

In addition to growing higher acre yields of crops and increasing the acreage of land that can be put to intensive agricultural use, there are important reserve possibilities for making what we already grow go farther as human food. This country is now operating on a livestock economy that provides us with an abundance of meat, eggs, and milk. However, the basic nutritional requirements of man could be met with a lower proportion of meat and milk than we now enjoy. Consequently, should it become necessary, the human-food potential of our cropland could be multiplied several times by a combined decrease in our animal-product diet and an increase in grain diet. Soybeans, common beans, peas, and peanuts can provide much of the necessary protein required to balance the larger amounts of high-carbohydrate grain, potatoes, and vegetables that would, as a result, be eaten.

Many other possibilities for increasing food production are yet to be more fully explored; some already are beginning to be employed in the more densely populated countries. Vegetables are being grown by tank-culture procedures on land that is not suitable for ordinary farming use. In other types of tank culture, waste cellulose and molasses are being converted into proteins by yeasts, with chemical fertilizers as the source of nitrogen and mineral nutrients. Blue-green algae are being grown in a similar manner, although they do not need to be supplied with readily available carbohydrate materials, since these materials are manufactured by the algae themselves. Much greater use, too, can be made of the food-producing potentialities of oceans, lakes, rivers, and reservoirs. Chemical fertilizers are highly effective in increasing the yield of fish in inland waters. And from the seas that surround us, possibilities are believed to exist in recovering plankton, a source of highly nutritious protein food.

Finally, there is great hope of being able to discover just how plants operate, by way of their chlorophyll, in the production of sugar out of the water absorbed by their roots and the carbon dioxide taken in through their leaves. Once this secret is exposed, we may be able to manufacture sugar at will; and from this sugar large-scale production of proteins and fats could readily be accomplished in the factory by microbial processes.

Assuming adequate supplies of push-button energy from petroleum, coal, and gas, from wind and falling water, from nuclear fission and fusion, and from the sun, we should be able to produce enough food in this country to feed 1 billion—1,000 million—people and to feed them well.

Byron T. Shaw has been administrator of the Agricultural Research Service of the United States Department of Agriculture since 1952. He directs the Department's complex program of research in all fields and coordinates federal and state research programs at the agricultural experiment stations at land-grant colleges and universities.

Dr. Shaw, a native of Utah, is a fellow of the American Society of Agronomy, the American Association for the Advancement of Science, and the Soil Science Society of America. He received the Department of Agriculture's Distinguished Service Award in 1955.

Research for Abundance

Byron T. Shaw

THE job of providing food for the future is getting bigger and harder. America's farmers are probably the most efficient in the world; their output has set records almost every year since World War II. Yet this fact remains: to meet the needs of 1975, *they must more than double their annual increases in output.*

Most of America's good farm land is already in use

and the farm labor force is diminishing, but the number of people who must be fed continues to increase and at an accelerated rate. The picture is, however, considerably brighter than these facts might at first indicate, for this smaller farm labor force, tilling the same acreage as now, will in 1975 produce *35 to 40 per cent more food, feed, and fiber*. This will be possible because of the results of research and the farmer's demonstrated willingness and ability to apply results as they are developed. If these farmers are to *double* their annual output increase, however, *research in agricultural sciences must be more productive than ever before*.

We are confident that such research, pursued vigorously and steadily, will measure up to the farmers' needs and thus to the needs of the increased populations of the future. Among the many reasons for this confidence are the knowledge of what research has already accomplished, the growing appreciation of its value both in and out of agriculture, and its increasing support by both state and Federal governments and by industry. Another reason, one perhaps basic to all others, is the organization for agricultural research that has been developed in this country over the last 75 years. This is a highly cooperative, closely knit organization, with programs involving state and Federal governments, private institutions, industry, and farmers. Its pattern of cooperation and acceptance of responsibility in attacking agricultural problems on a local, regional, and national basis is unique.

The state experiment stations are primarily concerned with problems related to the welfare of farmers and consumers within their respective states. The Federal Department of Agriculture has primary responsibility for research of regional and national scope. But most agricultural problems cut across state lines, and when they do, the Department and the state experiment stations join forces and share in the work. Most of the scientists of the Department of Agriculture are located at Federal field stations or at the state stations. State and Federal scientists operate in such close relationship that the work of each fits into an over-all pattern, the resulting accomplishments being those of a scientific team.

Industry, also, is an active member of this research organization. Although government-industry relationships are not as well defined as those of the state-Federal system, close research cooperation exists in many areas in which agriculture and industry have mutual interests. For example, there are strong cooperative ties in such specialized fields as agricultural chemicals, manufactured feeds, farm machinery, new products from agriculture or for agricultural use, and new methods of processing.

Rounding out this cooperative set-up are state and Federal research advisory committees, representing farmers, industry, scientists, and consumers. These committees are especially helpful in bringing problems to the attention of research administrators and in counseling with them as to which problems should have priority.

Industry accounts for roughly half of the funds invested in agricultural research. Federal and state governments share the other half about equally. Some 30 per cent of the funds appropriated by the Federal government go to the state experiment stations to become part of their research budgets.

This distinctively American system of agricultural research has been a powerful force in shaping our economy and is, in itself, one of our great national resources. In it lies our best hope for success in the job of providing food for the future. Recognition and support of research as a major national resource places a special obligation on research administrators and on scientists themselves to make sure that their approach is correct and that emphasis is given to those areas of research that will pay the highest long-term dividends.

When the great accomplishments of agricultural research are examined and traced to their sources, it is clearly apparent that the greatest progress has been made in those areas in which basic research has pointed the way. In planning our approach to the future, therefore, we must place greater emphasis on that aspect of research from which new scientific principles and new scientific methods will come. Only thus can agricultural science broaden the base of its knowledge and make its applied research more productive.

The need for more fundamental knowledge is apparent in all areas of agricultural research. It is particularly apparent, for example, in research on soils. In spite of all the efforts in conservation, the soils of the United States are, on the average, still deteriorating. Many farmers still have not adopted known soil-management practices that will give maximum yields on a sustained basis without depleting soil fertility. Before scientists can develop management practices that truly conserve the soil they must be able to characterize soils in relation to the plants growing on them. They must learn how to evaluate the effects of soil treatments in terms of both the changes these treatments cause in the soil and the influence of these treatments on plants. They must know what crops will grow best on a given soil under alternative systems of management.

There are two ways to go about this. The first, or empirical approach, is to conduct experiments on each soil, under each condition of temperature and rainfall, for each crop grown. Much of the research on soils has had to be carried on by this method, but it is almost a hopeless task when we consider the many soils and crops and the wide variety of climatic conditions in this country.

The second, or basic-research approach, is to develop methods of obtaining facts that will fit any soil anywhere. In this approach scientists must dig into the secrets of soil and plant. They must learn how nutrients move from the soil into the growing plant, how the plant uses these nutrients, and how temperature, moisture, and other environmental factors influence their availability to the plant. This approach is, of course, more difficult than the empirical one, and answers may not come quickly. But when the answers are found, when principles are established and methods discovered by which the needs for all crops on all soils under all conditions can be predicted, then it will be fairly easy to tell farmers how to handle their soils efficiently on a long-term basis.

In the years ahead, water—or the lack of it—may well determine the limit of crop production. The need for more efficient use of water is becoming increasingly apparent. Because of irrigation, more underground water is being removed in many areas of the West than is being returned through natural recharging. And too little is known about evaporation and transpiration to take full advantage of the water that is available. Can a practical means be found for artificially recharging ground water? How can a soil surface be conditioned to prevent or reduce evaporation? Can crop varieties be developed that will transpire less than those in use today? Questions like these can be answered only through fundamental studies that will provide new knowledge about soils, plants, water, and their interrelationships.

Another question that is waiting for an answer from basic research is: Can the number of plant species that will fix their own nitrogen be extended? The idea that nonleguminous plants might be nodulated has been a scientific teaser for more than 30 years. No one knows just how nitrogen is fixed biologically, although more is being learned about it each year. And the possibility that grasses, as well as corn and other crop plants, can be made to fix their own nitrogen is not so remote as it once seemed. The benefits in terms of increased efficiency of production that answers to these questions would bring would be tremendous.

A great deal of progress has been made and is being made in developing crop varieties that are resistant to disease and insect pests or adapted to specific climatic conditions. But, since plant breeders must go through the slow and tedious process of planting, selecting, crossing, and selecting again, it usually requires many years to develop a new variety and get it into one farmer's hands. The problem in developing such new varieties is that not enough is known about the plant itself or about the disease or insect attacking it. Why does a plant resist one disease and not another? What makes one plant stand up under an insect attack or to heat or drouth, and another go down? Only fundamental research can reveal what it is in the physiological make-up or the chemical constitution of a plant that makes it resistant to unfavorable factors in its environment.

An important clue to disease resistance was discovered recently when a simple inherited genetic resistance was found to one form of the infectious and cancerous avian leukosis complex in chickens. This discovery raises some fascinating questions: Does this simple form of genetic resistance operate against other forms of this disease or against other livestock diseases? Is there a similar genetic resistance character against insect pests or against heat and cold?

There are many unanswered questions about the mutations occurring in nature that increase the virulence of disease organisms, and about the relationships between weather conditions and the development and expression of disease. Equally important questions must be answered regarding insects. How do insects develop resistance to insecticides, and how can this resistance be overcome? How do temperature, rainfall, and other ecological factors favor the build-up of insect populations?

When basic research has provided answers to questions like these, applied research can go faster and farther in helping farmers provide food for our future. Investigations of this type are now under way in every area of agriculture. Some are in early stages, and no one can tell how remote the answers may be. Other studies have progressed to the point where practical applications are in sight or, in some cases, already in use. Basic research on plant-growth regulators, for example, is already paying off in the development of weed killers and defoliants, and in the development of chemicals to thin fruit blossoms or keep fruit on trees until picked, to root cuttings, and to prevent sprouting of potatoes in storage. All are the result of research that began more than 30 years ago with the discovery of the basic fact that certain chemicals can influence the growth behavior of plants.

Studies are now being made with gibberellic acid, a promising plant-growth regulator produced by a rice-disease fungus. About three years ago, scientists found that minute applications of this substance resulted in a greatly increased height and an earlier flowering of many kinds of plants. Gibberellic acid was soon being tested on a wide variety of crops and for a variety of purposes, including speeding the growth of trees for pulpwood; hastening germination of peas and lima beans under cold-temperature conditions; stimulating growth and improving palatability of forage crops; shortening the time required to produce seed of cabbage, kale, beets, carrots, and other biennial crops; and hastening early growth and fruiting of peach and citrus trees. Already scientists have progressed from the greenhouse to the field stage, and they are hopeful that, before too long, gibberellic acid can be more definitely recommended as another practical tool in agriculture.

The screwworm eradication program, now under way in the Southeastern states, has important potentialities for pay-off from basic research. Many years ago, scientists, using X rays to cause mutations in fruit flies, noticed that the flies were sometimes made sexually sterile by the radiations. Other studies were made of flight patterns, mating habits, population build-ups, and the life cycles of these insects. Among other discoveries it was found that a female screwworm fly mates only once during her lifetime; still other scientists, studying the nutrition of these insects, learned how to mass-produce them in the laboratory. Practical methods were consequently developed for sterilizing large numbers of screwworm flies with radioactive cobalt.

Putting all this information together, scientists came up with a promising method for eradicating the screwworm by releasing huge numbers of sterile males among the wild screwworm fly population. When this method was applied on Curaçao the screwworm was eliminated from the island. It is now being applied in Florida. Success in the eradication of this pest from the Southeast will effect savings of millions of dollars to livestock owners and will yield more meat and other livestock products for consumers.

The use of disease organisms to control insect pests is still another example of research that is beginning to pay big dividends. Fundamental studies have shown that insects, like other animals, are attacked by a variety of viruses, bacteria, fungi, protozoa, and nematodes, often with drastic reductions in their populations. A disease of the Japanese beetle, discovered through basic research, has been used for years to control this destructive pest of fruits, vegetables, and field crops. More recently, a virus has been put to use to control the alfalfa caterpillar.

Several years ago, a nematode-borne bacterial disease was discovered that, in preliminary tests, proved deadly to the codling moth, the corn earworm, the boll weevil, the pink bollworm, the white-fringed beetle, the vegetable weevil, and the cabbage worm. This disease-carrying nematode is now being studied under both laboratory and field conditions, and scientists are hopeful that it will provide still another weapon against the insect enemies of agriculture.

In these and in hundreds of other ways, agricultural research is helping to provide food for our future. But research also has an obligation to the present, and scientists cannot concentrate on problems in the future by neglecting those problems which farmers are facing now. Farmers are trying to find markets for their surplus products. They need research that will help them cut costs of production, balance supply with market demand, enhance the quality of their products, and improve their competitive position in the market place. It is the obligation of all agricultural scientists, whether in government or industry, to help them in every way possible to these ends.

The success of research in helping agriculture meet the demands of the times—whether it be 1960, 1975, or thereafter—depends on many factors. Certainly among the most important are adequate manpower and facilities and the cooperation of all those concerned with getting research results into practice. This is a job not only for the scientists themselves, but for legislators, educators, extension workers, farmers, and industry. Above all, it calls for the cooperation of the consuming public, who provide the funds and reap the benefits of agricultural research. Today's abundance is a result of research programs planned many years ago; tomorrow's abundance will depend on the researches that are being planned today.

Thomas A. Boyd, General Motors Research Staff consultant, is eminently qualified to write this article about Charles F. Kettering's studies of plant growth. Mr. Boyd is the author of Professional Amateur, *a biography of the late scientist and inventor who was so well known for his insatiable curiosity and his ability to inspire those with whom he worked. Mr. Boyd joined Mr. Kettering during World War I, assisted him in many projects at General Motors Research and was actively associated with him throughout his life. Mr. Kettering's death came before he was able to carry out his intention to write the article himself.*

Miracle of the Green Plant

Thomas A. Boyd

" JUST as long as the sun shines we don't need to worry about our food or fuel, if we'll get busy and learn how to convert that sunshine to chemical energy.... If we starve to death or run out of fuel, it's our own fault."

In this 1948 comment, the late Charles F. Kettering recognized that every week our earth receives in sunshine more energy than is stored in all our coal, petroleum, natural gas, oil shale, and tar sands. He knew, too, that vegetation captures on the average only about one-tenth of 1 per cent, or one part in a thousand, of the vast energy the sun sends down to us. If we could learn how to catch and hold only *two*-tenths of 1 per cent of the energy out of that wealth of sunshine, Kettering declared, our food supply would be doubled. "If we don't succeed in catching at least that much, it is because we are a little stupid in the attic.... And I don't think we are that bad."

"The great receiving set for this solar energy is the leaf of the plant," said Kettering, "and if it wasn't for that you wouldn't be here.... Nature has devised a means in the plant of taking two low-energy compounds, carbon dioxide and water, with energy from the sun, to build our entire plant life in all its variations. She did this long before man was in existence." And she does it "without a test tube, without a burette, without a chemical balance, without a log table or a slide rule, or anything else. In fact, nature never had a college education.... Yet, today, in this age in which we call ourselves scientific, we know very little about how the leaf of a plant is able to pick up the radiant energy from the sun and convert it into new chemical compounds."

This is "a miracle," and "the most important single thing in the world. It is the only way we have of keeping some of the sun's energy down here so we can use it next winter when it gets cold.... One may say that this is one of the things the Lord never intended us to find out about. Well, He is certainly not trying to keep it secret, because He has it around everywhere."

Kettering felt it our business to find out how this was done, but "So far as our own country is concerned, we don't have to hurry about it." He did not think a shortage of food or fuel in America was going to come quickly, although this was not the good fortune of some other countries. Nevertheless they, and someday we ourselves, are going to have to learn more about how to catch and store this energy from the sun. And years before we make use of its results, research on the problem must be started: "Research is something which if you don't undertake until you have to, it is too late. It is just as though you waited to see the smoke rolling out of a building before calling a fire insurance agent."

Nearly 30 years ago, as the first activity of the then newly formed Charles F. Kettering Foundation, Kettering, out of an understanding of this circumstance and in his vital interest in the miracle of the green leaf, set up an investigation of photosynthesis and chlorophyll at Antioch College in Yellow Springs, Ohio. "Photosynthesis and chlorophyll" are big words, he said. They sound "as though we must be a smart bunch of fellows. When we say photosynthesis, we say the effect of light. And chlorophyll is the Greek word for green leaf. But we don't know a bit more about the green leaf in Greek than we do in English—not a bit.... So I told the boys, 'Let's make it simple. We will just ask the question: why is the grass green?' "

In setting up that research Kettering did not expect to find out quickly how the green leaf captures and stores up the energy of the sun: "We have to recognize that now we are just learning how to learn." But he did think that within 10 years or so they might at least know where the problem lay. Half jokingly and half seriously he advised the young men who were undertaking the research "to get married and have a lot of children, because I think this is about a three-generation job. I shall not be disappointed if I have to die without knowing, because I think some generation soon will know."

The investigations that he and other researchers in the field pursued throughout the years did add materially to our knowledge of how nature performs her great miracle. And up until his death in November, 1958, he remained optimistic about the finding of an answer to the question, Why is the grass green?

In an expression of his boundless optimism about what the future could be, Kettering, late in life, commented: "You can have anything, no matter what it is, if you have imagination and a genuine desire to have it. You've got to work and continue to strive for what you hope to attain, and be patient.... If you keep your mind on the job, have faith in yourself and others, there is nothing we can dream about that we can't have."

After Kettering retired in 1947 from his many years as head of research for General Motors, he set up a solar energy research laboratory, also at Yellow Springs, Ohio. There, with a staff of about 30 persons, he energetically pursued the search for a better and more efficient way to capture the energy of sunshine. And, through the Charles F. Kettering Foundation— of which his son, Eugene W. Kettering, is chairman of the board of trustees—his program of research in that field continues under the direction of Dr. Howard A. Tanner.

"There is no reason why we cannot convert sunshine without growing plants," said Kettering. "We looked at birds until we learned how to fly. But there aren't any feathers on airplanes."

He even thought that there was something of a parallel between man's realization of the age-old dream of flight and what remains to be done toward the better utilization of the sun's energy. "It is difficult now to picture the state of mind of the people of fifty years ago, ten years before the coming of the airplane," he remarked in 1943. "A common expression of the day was, 'You might as well try to *fly* as to do that.' For hundreds of years, man had dreamed of mechanical flight and even written poems about it. I wonder how many people remember Darius Green and his Flying Machine. To fly was the ambition of the ages. But, as the result of hundreds of failures, formulas had been developed and books written to prove that man could not fly.

"Although a smoke screen had been thrown around the entire subject to hide these failures to fly, two men in Dayton, Ohio, . . . experimented with kites and gliders and finally put a gasoline engine of their own make in an airplane. They used calculations to find out how it could be done and not why it was impossible. And they flew right through the smoke screen of impossibility."

It was Kettering's firm belief that, out of the persistent effort of many devoted investigators, someone someday would break through a similar smoke screen of impossibility by finding a way to make a great deal more of the sun's infinite supply of energy available for food—and for fuel as well. In the years just prior to his death he found this confidence fortified by the encouraging progress in solar energy research.

"Much has been said about the depletion of our soil," Kettering noted in his 1946 presidential address to the American Association for the Advancement of Science. "This is a scientific problem of long standing. I believe that, if necessity demands, we can go to our inexhaustible supply of minerals in the sea for all the plant food we will ever need to keep our farm land productive, just as we have gone to the air for nitrogen. Only about $2\frac{1}{2}$ per cent of the weight of a plant is mineral.

"We have learned how to obtain salts and bromine from the sea commercially. To obtain millions of pounds of bromine annually from sea water is an important chemical development of the past 25 years. There is one pound of bromine to about eight tons of sea water.

"What are the chemical reserves of the sea? Each cubic mile of sea water contains 90 million tons of chlorine, 53 million tons of sodium, 5,700,000 tons of magnesium, 4,300,000 tons of sulphur, 3,300,000 tons of potassium, 2,400,000 tons of calcium, 310,000 tons of bromine, and lesser quantities of many other elements, including trace elements. There are 320 million cubic miles of sea water. Here is a real challenge to future generations to become chemists and engineers of the sea."

In this atomic age one may ask whether someday it may not be possible to use atomic energy in obtaining our food and fuel. The answer, of course, is yes. Nature has always used atomic energy for that purpose, for that is just what sunshine is. It is energy radiated to the earth from that eternal fire made by the "fusing" of hydrogen into helium up there in the sun.

"The front of development is not a straight line," observed Kettering out of his long experience in research. "It is a very ragged line.... Since none of us is smart enough to arrive directly at the final result, we must work our way very laboriously from experiment to experiment and from test to test until we finally get there. A lot of people don't want to do this. They would like to find a short cut for the tedious trying and failing of experimentation. They think they are smart enough or educated enough to get the result directly."

The fact is "we think we are further along the path of knowledge than we actually are."

It was his view that "a certain amount of intelligent ignorance is essential to progress; for, if you know too much, you won't try the thing.... One thing that is likely to be overlooked in the solution of a problem is that theorizing is not nearly as effective as trying.... We should not be either ashamed or afraid to make intelligent mistakes," he said. "The greatest mistake of all is to do nothing."

Kettering recognized, of course, that finding a better way to capture the energy of sunshine is a difficult problem. But a difficult problem was, in his estimation, merely one that is not understood; failure to understand is the *reason* it is difficult, and the degree of difficulty reflects the magnitude of the ignorance. But we are prone to blame the difficulty on the problem, like those who speak of "incurable" diseases. And "the only incurable diseases," Kettering declared, "are those the doctors don't know how to cure. I don't believe the Lord ever put in His deck any 'jokers' like incurable diseases."

Never was there a man with more faith in what patience and persistence can accomplish in the search for new knowledge. This too was founded on his own long experience. "It doesn't matter if you try and try and try again, and fail," he once said to some of those working with him. "It does matter if you try and fail, and fail to try again.... It is the 'follow-through' that makes the great difference between failure and ultimate success, for it is so easy to stop.... Failures, repeated failures, are finger posts on the road to achievement.... The only time you don't want to fail is the last time you try."

The trouble is that we emphasize the difficulties all the time, Kettering pointed out in a further expression of his principles of progress. We can overcome difficulties "if we want to.... Aladdin's Lamp was a story, of course. But there is a psychological principle back of that which is this, that when you keep on wishing (and working) for a thing, you get it."

We have, to date, "chipped away a few fragments from the Mountain of Knowledge—fragments that have changed our entire way of life," Kettering commented in 1955. "But looming ahead of us, practically intact, lies a huge mass of fundamental facts, any one of which, if uncovered, could change our civilization. In that mountain lies the solution to the problem of how we can utilize the practically limitless energy of the sun pouring down on the earth, and there also is the answer to the age-old problem of feeding the millions of undernourished people in the world."

"If we can learn how to convert sunshine without growing plants we may be able to make the vital step toward abundance and peace," he wrote shortly before he died. "There will then be nothing to fight about." And "the greatest thing this generation can do," he said earlier, "is to lay a few steppingstones for the next generation."

Clifford M. Hardin has been chancellor of the University of Nebraska since 1954. Prior to his association with the University, he was dean of agriculture and director of the agricultural experiment station at Michigan State University.

Dr. Hardin is a native of Indiana. He studied at Purdue University and at the University of Chicago, and received his Ph.D. from Purdue in 1941. He was awarded an honorary degree of Doctor of Science by Purdue in 1952, and an honorary degree of Doctor of Laws by Creighton University in 1956, and was elected president of the American Association of Land-Grant Colleges and State Universities in 1960.

New Horizons in Education

Clifford M. Hardin

IF there is any one, big, common denominator in America's hopes, problems, challenges, and opportunities, that common denominator is education. In our nation, education has its share in every significant achievement, problem, hope, and challenge that comes into focus on the economic, social, or spiritual scene. For those who participate in our educational effort, this is one of the most exciting facts of American life.

At this particular time, higher education finds itself holding a spotlight of attention. Gradually, as a nation, we have come to understand that our destiny is being shaped to a great degree by how well our colleges and universities can do their respective jobs during the next 25 to 50 years. This understanding prevails whether the subject under consideration deals with agriculture, industry, international affairs, racial understanding, or any of the other important facets of our society.

When we relate this concept to the future of American agriculture, the following conclusions take form: (1) Higher education has been a major factor in the amazing and tremendous developments that have taken place in the American production of food and fiber. (2) Higher education faces a great challenge and a great opportunity in the role of helping American agriculture progress and adjust itself amid an explosive population increase and an eruption of new information, techniques, and methods in a world atmosphere charged with pressure for change. Thus, it is well to stop and consider a few points pertinent to the nature of higher education in America, to the direction in which it should move, and to some of the ways in which that movement might be accomplished.

As a starting point, we need to recognize that it is

now impossible to separate "an agricultural education" from the whole process of American higher education. Our national life has become so complex and its various aspects so interwoven that it is absurd simply to label a man as "a farmer" and assume that identification to be adequate. The old, popular, rustic image that once took form at the mention of the word "farmer" has long since become obsolete. The old notion of the farm family as an isolated group engaged in a pastoral life of sowing, tending, and harvesting is as unrealistic today as a quill pen in a modern accounting department.

We need to recognize, too, that higher education has played an important role in the transition that has taken place in agriculture. Responsible in large measure for the remarkably effective influence of higher education in this change is the fact that, contrary to some popular notions, "agricultural education" in this country has developed not outside the orbit of higher education generally but as an integral part of it.

One of the unique accomplishments of our higher education has been the successful fusing of all professional education, including agriculture, with the basic, mainstream effort in the arts, sciences, and humanities. This is truly a major achievement and we can take justifiable pride in the fact that it is distinctly an American development. In no other part of the world do educational systems exist which afford the intercommunication of ideas and disciplines that is found in the United States. And we can take some satisfaction, too, in the fact that it is a development which is being both praised and emulated elsewhere.

Our agricultural colleges, whether they began as separate institutions or as parts of universities, have concerned themselves with much more than specific technical training in the science of agriculture. In one way or another all of them have offered their students some significant solid study in the liberal arts. Those agricultural colleges that are parts of universities have had their students take advantage of courses offered by the associated college of arts and sciences; those that exist as separate institutions have managed to build arts and sciences subject courses into their own curriculums.

This development, which has given breadth and depth to our programs of agricultural education, has proved to be highly important both to society as a whole and to those engaged directly in agricultural pursuits. It has tended to keep instructional standards high and has prevented a possible drift of agricultural education toward the level of trade-school training. It has helped to provide a broad base for the research and experimental programs that have flourished in our colleges of agriculture. It has helped to give American agriculture a recognized status above that accorded to agriculture in many parts of the world. It has given leaders to American agriculture who can hold their own with leaders in business, industry, and other fields. But most important of all, it is a development through which students of agriculture are considered first as people and only secondarily as human resource material vital to the revolutionary progress of American agriculture.

How did this development come about? Did it come about because our American forefathers had an unusually clear and deep appreciation of the importance of agriculture in a growing society? This may have been a factor, but primarily this development is a natural consequence of the inherent American belief in the dignity—the importance—of the individual citizen and in his right to an opportunity to develop his abilities and talents to their greatest capacity.

This fundamental concept is in sharp contrast to that which places first importance upon the attainment of a specific production goal or upon the accomplishment of a preset economic standard within a given period of time. It is a concept that places emphasis on service to people rather than on service to plans or programs, a concept that has made America great in the eyes of the world because of its kinship with the whole American notion of freedom.

The great challenge and the great opportunity of higher education today lie in the task of continuing and expanding this warm, and human, and *right* concept in the service of tomorrow's needs and problems. This applies to all areas of our society, including education in agriculture. To meet the challenge and realize the opportunity require progress in at least three general spheres.

The first of these can be defined, in general, as the sphere of educational understanding. One of the phenomenal aspects of the popularity of education, especially higher education in America, is that it has been attained without a clear understanding of the nature and principal purpose of education.

That higher education is popular is indicated by ever-increasing college enrollments and by the expanding proportion of high school graduates who now go on to college. But there is no convincing indication that either students or parents see higher education in the same light as educators. Most colleges and universities conceive their programs as opportunities for students to participate in a continuing intellectual experience. Yet a great many people (judging from frequent comments) look upon education more as a commodity than as an intellectual experience, something that will be good for the pay check, good for business, good for agriculture, good for the national defense, and so on. For these objectives, education will, indeed, serve good purpose, but its first concern must be the development of the student as a person. Without the attainment of a closer understanding of the nature and purpose of a higher education, we are increasingly running the risk, as Dr. John W. Gardner, president of the Carnegie Corporation of New York, said recently, of having education "accepting trivial assignments, of playing technician when it should be playing statesman."

The responsibility for bringing about such an understanding in those who support education and those who are served by it does not rest with educators alone. It is the responsibility of each of the various components of our society: farm groups, labor groups, industrialists, businessmen, and people in government and in professional life.

Second, we need to give increased attention to the operational sphere of education. If education is con-

cerned with human beings who struggle continuously
to penetrate new frontiers and solve new problems, the
educational effort can, thus, never become an operation that is stabilized. It never has become such an
operation in America, but if education is to fulfill its
responsibilities, a greater adherence to this concept
must be demonstrated internally by educational institutions and externally by the society that supports them.

This means that agricultural colleges must be willing
to face up to changes in curriculum, in methods of
making maximum use of agricultural extension agents,
in providing leadership for adjustments in high school
vocational agricultural instruction, and in broadening
the horizons of research and experimentation. Happily,
in all these areas, the trend is toward greater emphasis
on fundamentals and greater encouragement for the
imaginative, the daring, and the bold. The speed with
which change has come to agriculture during the past
half century has conditioned our colleges of agriculture
to the acceptance of change and has given them experience in detecting the difference between change per se
and progress.

It would serve no useful purpose to minimize the
dimensions of the internal task with which educational
institutions are faced. With staff shortages, enlarged

student bodies, and financial difficulties, education becomes an increasingly difficult, though by no means hopeless, task.

The segments of our American society outside our colleges of agriculture that look to these institutions for leadership, guidance, and help are more numerous today than they were less than 100 years ago when land-grant institutions were being established. The "ag college" is no longer an institution whose activities are a matter of interest to the farmer exclusively. To those farmers these institutions once served have come the thousands of enterprises which now compose the sprawling empire of "agribusiness." Many others have discovered that their special interests in nutrition, in economics, in medical research, in chemistry, and in a whole conglomerate of other efforts are also involved in the "ag college" program. All these partners in the broad pursuit of agricultural education have roles to fulfill in the years ahead. Colleges will have increasing need for their help and certainly for their support and perhaps most of all for their clear recognition that the college community is not a factory but rather an unique place of free inquiry, teaching, and searching for new knowledge.

The third sphere in need of attention is that of educational expansion. In the realm of education, America has never wanted for frontiers. And now there is the great frontier of "continuing education." Higher education seems destined to play a major role in its development, and because of their experience in extension work and their commitment to the maintenance of broad educational opportunity, agricultural institutions are well qualified to lead the way.

The concept of continuing education, now taking root in America, is a systematic and professional effort to help people make the most of their abilities. It is a sound movement which is taking form in response to two fundamental concepts: (1) since education is a continuing process, it merits a continuing opportunity for participation, and (2) the modern needs for education and training cannot be filled by one stint of "schooling," even if it includes college.

Continuing-education programs are being designed to make systematic learning a lifetime habit. Through a variety of educational projects—conferences, institutes, special intensive training sessions, postgraduate clinics, and short courses—its aim is to serve both young people and adults. Centers for continuing education have already been opened at several universities and more are in the process of building. But the erection of these physical facilities is only a beginning. In the final analysis the success of the effort will depend on the content of the programs and the people who conduct them. It is here that the nature of the challenge to our colleges and universities comes into focus.

To be of maximum benefit, programs of continuing education must develop as integral parts of the total university effort and make full use of faculty personnel. Here the staff of the agricultural college can be of great help. These people, who are accustomed to participating in extension work, can be the bellwethers who can serve their academic colleagues as leaders in a program of continuing education.

The problem of enlisting widespread university staff participation in continuing education is not altogether an intra-institutional responsibility. Development in colleges and universities in this country has proceeded pretty much along the lines that the people who support them would have them develop. Leaders of these institutions have resisted—and rightfully so—those suggestions which, in their judgment, threatened academic standards and freedom of academic pursuits. But our universities and colleges have not insisted on going their own ways exclusively; they have remained sensitive both to the wishes and to the needs of the people they serve.

Thus, as higher education moves into the expanded function of continuing education, it needs encouragement from outside its immediate precincts. Fortunately, that encouragement has been forthcoming. Business and industry, as well as agriculture, are continually demonstrating a willingness to cooperate in the establishment and operation of adult educational programs. The need for in-service training programs, for postgraduate short courses, and for programs designed to help with the effective use of increasing leisure time and to serve the increasing number of people who are now living long beyond retirement age—all of these *needs* are gaining recognition. The immediate task is to convert the *idea* of continuing education into a functioning *program,* and this requires help from within and from without our educational institutions.

By way of summary, these three general spheres of progress merit emphasis. First, our approach to the solution of agricultural problems must, of necessity, be broad. Education can and will assist the development of capable people who, in turn, will have the responsibility of attacking specific problems in depth.

But our educational institutions must not be turned into a national chain of "fix-it" shops to deal with every individual problem that arises. Education's prime responsibility is to people, and its contribution toward the solution of problems must be through people, not around them.

Second, the educational record in this country merits confidence for the future. It is a record in which educational institutions have been brought closer to the rank and file without depriving the unusually gifted of ample opportunity to pursue learning at an accelerated rate. In short, although our educational effort needs some adjustment, some replacement of emphasis, and considerable expansion, it does not need rebuilding.

Third, American education faces the greatest opportunity and perhaps the greatest test of its history in the years immediately ahead. The degree to which it succeeds will depend to a great extent on its ability to serve vastly increased numbers of people with all of the intellectual competence, human understanding, honesty, and dignity that characterizes the good teacher.

Herrell F. DeGraff is Babcock Professor of Food Economics at Cornell University. He received his Ph.D. from Cornell in 1941, after majoring in agricultural economics.

Among the subjects he has taught during his career at Cornell are farm management, agricultural marketing, and land economics. He also has supervised Cornell's farm cost-accounting projects and has served as the elected faculty representative on the board of trustees.

Dr. DeGraff was consultant to the Rockefeller Foundation on its agricultural development programs in Mexico and in Colombia.

Management of
Land, Labor and Capital

Herrell F. DeGraff

TWO of my neighbors are poultrymen—egg producers. One has 10,000 hens in a new building laid out and equipped for the closest possible approach to automatic operation. Feeding, watering, house cleaning and egg gathering are so efficiently arranged that, exclusive of sorting and casing the eggs, care of the 10,000 birds barely keeps one man busy.

The other neighbor has roughly the same number of hens on four floors of a converted dairy barn. Although material-handling and work routines have been developed with care, the arrangement of the building is a handicap, at least in comparison with the new facilities on my other neighbor's farm. And, again exclusive of egg handling, the 10,000 birds in this building require twice as many hours of labor as those on the first farm. Given equal performance by the hens, the quantity of eggs in return for a day's work is thereby cut in half.

Circumstances that appear to be insignificant sometimes are found to have a marked effect on our thinking. For example, take the order of words in the title of this chapter. It is the order that first came to mind when the writing of this paper was suggested. But ask an economist about the factors of production (the cost items used in production) and he typically will answer "land, labor, and capital," and add, as a fourth and separate factor, "management." Yet, in practice, management obviously comes at the beginning of the list, not at the end. Management is a combining function, it is the decision-making process that determines how the other cost factors will be used.

In farming, what should be the order of the other three factors? The appropriate sequence is not "land, labor, and capital" but "labor, capital, and land." Perhaps the latter is not as euphonious, not as easy to say, but the thinking about economic problems of farm families would be much clearer if this were the order in which these factors were considered.

Others have discussed in this book the number of people that our agriculture will be able to feed in the future, and the outlook they project is an optimistic one. The advance of technology, the forward march of chemical farming, and the contributions of genetics, physiology, and pathology promise to keep the nation abundantly supplied with products from the soil as far ahead as anyone can see or can reasonably speculate. Moreover, progress with petroleum-powered and electrically powered equipment will permit the work to be done by fewer farmers. These justifiably optimistic views indicate that the challenge for agriculture lies in a different direction. How the farm family can achieve a level of living—a total of comforts, conveniences, and satisfactions—at least equal to that of families in other economic pursuits is the real challenge. It poses the question of how the individual farm family can be assured that the annual value of its products, with an adequate margin between selling price and production cost, is sufficient to earn a comparable net return.

Family labor—the work done by the farm operator and members of his family—represents about three-quarters of the total labor force in American agriculture. So commonly is a farm thought of simply as an operation for selling produce that the facts of the picture are often overlooked. Actually operator and family labor are being sold; they are being sold in the form of crop and livestock products. About 95 per cent of American farms are family-operated units, farms intended to provide both home and livelihood for the families on them. The farm should thus be thought of as the means of providing the family with a job, and it is their own labor that is the major commodity most families have to sell. A fully employed farm operator is the nearest approach to a fixed unit that can be found in the farm operation; what his labor and his family's labor produces in a year is the prime determinant of how good a job has been provided for them by the farm.

If it takes one man no more hours to care for 10,000 hens than another man requires for half that number, the return for his work is almost certain to be higher.

But if he has to invest money in a different kind of building and more equipment in order to handle the larger number of hens, he is faced with the question of how the cost of the needed additional capital outlay compares with the cost of the additional labor that otherwise would be required to get the job done.

Presumably the farmer and his family cannot themselves do the work for which they lay out cash to hire labor. If they could do the work and still hire it done, someone else would get that part of the labor return from the farm. Or, if they hire labor to do the work which they might be able to do with different buildings and equipment, then they face the question of comparative costs of the additional capital and the hired labor. It is the purpose of a farm to support the operator and his family, and how well it does this is determined primarily by how effectively the family uses its own labor in turning out products for sale. This is why management of labor must be a first consideration if a farm operation is to be effective.

To use labor effectively, the farmer obviously must have tools as up-to-date and as perfectly tailored to the work load on his farm as it is possible for him to have. And the tools should be acquired in an order that successively removes the peak points of pressure on the labor force throughout the year. The acquisition of a tool that can only save labor at a time of year when there is little work to be done should have a very low priority in comparison to a tool that can save labor at the busiest season.

Capital represented by tools is nothing more than an alternative to capital represented by labor; in addition to the principle of cutting off labor peaks, a farmer's objective should be to achieve that combination of labor and equipment that gives him *in toto* the lowest cost. This goal emphasizes a major management problem. The farmer must have the appropriate tools to permit him to work effectively, but at the same time he must avoid an acquisition of tools that could not be economically justified. On one farm a several-thousand-dollar piece of equipment might earn a high return, on another it might better be custom-rented, while on a third the greatest gain might lie in eliminating the crop that requires the tool. This is only to say that this labor-equipment balance—which really is a labor-capital balance—has come to be one of the toughest management problems on most farms.

Note also that, in this sense, service buildings— granaries, cattle sheds, chicken houses, and the like— are just as much production tools as are tractors, plows, and sprayers. Outmoded cow barns, which almost force a farmer into a wasteful use of labor, are as much a handicap as outmoded mules and hoes. The amount of capital that improved buildings or modern equipment can absorb is almost endless. Thus the management problem centers on the question of which dollar of capital outlay is justified and will more than earn its way and which one is no more than a luxury that good management can avoid.

One of the most critical problems in connection with the proper use of capital invested in equipment is to have the productive use of each piece of equipment great enough to justify its cost. A four-row corn planter in a two-row patch of corn is absurd, but the principle applies in like manner to every dollar invested in every machine and every service building. The farmer who gets greater-capacity tools, in order to plow or plant or harvest an acre more quickly, has merely equipped himself out of part of his job—unless he also has acres enough to keep himself otherwise busy. If he also equipped the hired man out of a job, he and his family might be much better off, but if only his own productive work is displaced, acquisition of the equipment is questionable, unless of course, he rents or purchases additional land on which to use it.

Whether to buy land or rent from another owner constitutes another of the most complex problems in agriculture and one that requires an appropriate answer. Often the answer will be a completely different one for different farmers. One reason that land prices have continued to move up throughout the postwar years is that so many farmers have found it advantageous to acquire additional land to make their farms adequate. This is typically the case where additional capital is laid out for land to justify the capital already laid out for equipment. As more effective tools continue to be developed—to apply to farm jobs not yet mechanized or to replace less efficient tools now in use —this problem of an appropriate balance between tools and land will continue to burden the manager of most farms.

Then, to continue our sequence, how does good management get the most out of land resources? Again this is a problem of effective use of capital—capital invested in seed, in fertilizer, and in other production supplies. And again it is the use of capital to justify previously invested capital.

If all this indicates that farming already is a complex business and will be increasingly complex in the future, that is precisely what we have intended it to show.

Just as today's farming is different from that of a generation ago, tomorrow's farming will be fully as different from today's.

Agriculture is already one of the most highly capitalized businesses in America, in terms of the capital investment required to permit one farm worker to be fully effective. As the employment of capital has increased, in all its many applications, the complexity of the management problem in agriculture has increased, and it will continue to increase in the years to come. The tools and equipment—bigger, better, and more costly—will still be essential if the farmer and his family are to produce effectively. And these factors will force an increase in the average amount of land per farm, for maximum production from the land will continue to be imperative. Thus, capital in tools will require capital in land, and the capital in land will require still more capital for most effective use of the land.

But the main purpose of it all will be to make farm-family labor sufficiently productive to permit the farm family to live as other contemporary American families live.

Richard C. McCurdy has been president of Shell Chemical Company since 1953. A native of Iowa, he joined Shell in 1933 upon his graduation from Stanford University in Palo Alto, Calif. He was elected board chairman of the Manufacturing Chemists' Association in 1960.

Shell Chemical Company was one of the early pioneers in the development of petroleum chemicals for use in agriculture, and today is one of the leading companies in the field of agricultural and industrial chemicals.

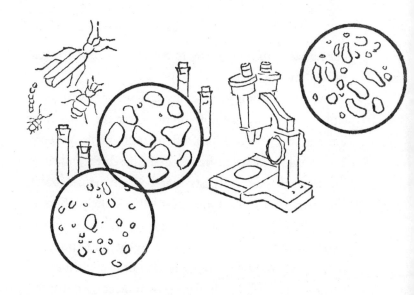

Insect, Disease and Weed Control

Richard C. McCurdy

POSSIBLY no one has ever seen a completely healthy plant. Few crops are spared the indignity of being either devoured by insects, or attacked by other enemies, or crowded out by weeds. It is well for our peace of mind that our domesticated crop plants have not been able to cry out with pain when sick or wounded. Had this been so, compassion would have moved us to develop much earlier than we did the protective and healing measures that only came with

67

our necessity to produce more food more efficiently and in the amount needed.

There is nothing strange, mysterious, or new in principle in what we are now doing. Over the years since Pasteur, the medical profession, with noble purpose, hard work, and scientific methods, has been endeavoring to overcome the pests that bedevil man. Modern chemistry is the doctor's great ally; it helps him to understand the processes that go on inside us and to know what our diet should be, what antiseptics we should use, and what complex chemical medicines can best be employed in regulating or protecting our internal functions. Chemical tools are being used similarly to cure the ills of all the living things on which we depend for food and fiber, with the care that safely guards against any possible harmful effects on human health. These chemicals have already protected large acreages of crops against destruction by parasites, and they offer still greater promise in the years ahead.

During the early stages of the development of a new product for agricultural use, the public tends to exaggerate successes and failures. Most of the scientists directly concerned, however, occupy a conservative middle ground, humble before the complexities of the problem, highly conscious of their responsibilities, but confident of ultimate success. They know that food is the primary essential of life, and they propose to do something constructive to the end that future generations will not suffer from any lack of it.

Agricultural progress can be roughly divided into three eras: the "blood, sweat, and tears" period of manual labor that went on for centuries; the mechanical revolution that started about 100 years ago with the McCormick reaper, followed by the power tractor, the electric motor, and other labor-saving devices; and the modern era in which the efforts of man and machines are now being facilitated by chemicals, including fertilizers, pesticides, and growth regulators.

Today, the chemical era is just beginning. Farmers are using hundreds of millions of pounds of scientifically designed chemicals that make it possible to control plant diseases, kill grasshoppers, destroy nematodes, stimulate poultry to a more rapid growth, and accomplish many other feats that better agricultural production. Many of these chemicals did not even exist prior to World War II; and a host of new wonders are now in the chemical laboratories or in the field-testing stage.

Let us examine some of the diverse activities of the chemists, look briefly at some of their accomplishments, and speculate a little on what the future may have in store. First let us consider the war against the insect world, next the control of harmful soil organisms, then the destruction of weeds, after which we shall talk about growth regulators, fungicides, and rat killers.

Ecology, or the marvelously complex balance of nature, is the equilibrium condition toward which nature relentlessly moves if left alone. But this natural balance is radically upset by the mere act of farming. A clean, cultivated, healthy field of hybrid corn, for example, is about as far away from the natural balance of the vegetation that preceded it in the wild state as one can imagine. Mankind crossed this bridge long ago and there is no going back. So we go forward with the purpose of effecting a new ecological balance that offers more food and fiber for the benefit of the human race.

The first and obvious step to more and better food is to stop the needless destruction of the crops that are being produced. Insects eat a third of all we grow, at an estimated cost of some 4 billion dollars per year. If this waste could be eliminated, we would have 50 per cent more produce for human consumption. It takes a lot of hard work to develop an insecticide that will dispatch the insects on a food crop economically and not interfere with its value for food purposes. But it is no more difficult to accomplish this than to develop a good medicine, and both goals are being realized regularly.

To conclude, however, that the few insecticides now produced will permanently dispose of the insect problem is to reckon without a knowledge of the staying power of the enemy. Some 350 million years ago this was an insect world. When the first mammals appeared, they, no doubt, were bitten, parasitized, and even killed by waiting insects; and leaves and fruits were probably crawling with ants, caterpillars, and beetles. When man arrived on the scene, the mosquitoes may have been waiting for him. And he may have often had to walk for days to find grain and fruit that had not been devoured by the annual locust invasion. For all we know, in a few more minutes of geologic time man may be gone. But it is a good bet that, in the dull red twilight of a dying sun, one of the final bits of life on earth will be some tiny insect. Some of the insects that were here when man arrived on the scene may still be here after he has departed.

Modern insecticidal materials, of which the principal examples have been developed since the war, are versatile, effective, and flexible. They can be tailored to a particular crop, pest, and condition of application. Some are long-lasting, whereas others are made to disappear promptly if that seems desirable. And a little goes a long way: 1 to 4 ounces of a good insecticide can often protect a whole acre of a growing crop against some parasite that is attacking it. Without such insecticides, farmers cannot raise the food we now need, let alone that required for the vastly increased number of mouths we must expect to feed by 1975.

We obviously have some fine weapons with which to wage our war against insects, but the enemy has a formidable counterdefense in the rapid reproductive powers that have kept it going since it first came into being. As in ages past, insects effectively roll with the punch and, in time, change genetically to resist any new threat. This resistance is one of the major challenges that entomological science faces today. Some 60 species of insects have become more or less resistant to one or more insecticides. Thus, on top of the elaborate research that goes into the development of better insecticides by usual methods, considerable effort has to be directed toward an understanding of the fundamental physiology and genetics of insect resistance.

A bang-up solution to the resistance problem might

save a lot of work and money, but failure to solve this particular problem will not mean we have lost the food battle. The brilliant strides in insecticide research since the war have put us well out in front of our insect enemies. One of the principal reasons that we still lose 4 billion dollars worth of farm produce a year to the insect world is that we have not fully employed the weapons already at hand. And, as long as we vigorously continue our research efforts, new insecticidal weapons will likely continue to be created faster than the insect pests can develop resistance against the old ones.

Food crops do not constitute the only front upon which we are attacked by insect pests. As carriers of such diseases as malaria, elephantiasis, and sleeping sickness they are equally harmful to us. Despite the substantial advances already made against it, malaria, carried by the anopheles mosquito, is estimated to have killed one man or woman every 15 seconds during 1956. But these are only a few of the problems into which we must probe more deeply.

If plants suddenly stood on their heads and waved their roots in the surrounding air, even farmers would be amazed at the extent and density of the resulting aerial jungle. We traditionally protect and nurture the parts of plants that are above ground, but our attitude toward their roots has been too much a case of out of sight out of mind—and often out of kilter.

Every clod of earth teems with many different forms of minute plant and animal life, known collectively as the edaphon of the soil. This edaphon includes the slime molds, bacteria, fungi, yeasts, algae, protozoa, rotifers, tardigrades, nematodes, mollusks, symphyllios, mites, and soil insects. It is probably more complex than the plankton of the sea. Many of these exist at the expense of plant roots. Modern agricultural science has only begun to appreciate the seriousness of these unseen attacks and to do something about them. They are no less critical than the attacks of insects, diseases, and weeds on the visible parts of plants.

Our modern concept of the edaphon is one of natural balance between harmful and beneficial organisms. The beneficial types of bacteria, yeasts, and fungi in the soil break down plant residues, releasing their nutrients; many of them are also the natural enemies of other types of organisms that are harmful to plants. Some soil fumigants that are not in themselves highly toxic to plant parasites benefit the afflicted crop plant simply by tipping the balance in the edaphon in favor of the beneficial types of organisms. For instance, in controlling the deadly oak-root fungus, fumigation succeeds by killing an organism that is the natural enemy of another fungus, *Trichoderma;* the *Trichoderma,* relieved of its parasites, then obligingly disposes of *its* enemy, the oak-root fungus.

Whole fields of plants can wither overnight, with their roots rotted off at the ground line. Beans, peas, tomatoes, melons, and cucumbers may be attacked by parasites shortly after fruiting begins; other plants, less acutely ill, may be debilitated and thus become easy prey for pests. Such troubles are often caused by various species of microbes that inhabit the soil and are largely due, it is believed, to imbalance in the edaphon. This edaphon thus becomes a very necessary and promising area of research, albeit a complex one. Some effective fungicidal soil fumigants are known now, but much remains to be done. Development of plants that are resistant both to insect and disease offers inviting possibilities.

It is difficult to assess the extent of the damage done by nematodes; doubtless much of it is as yet unrecognized. These tiny worms, of which at least 200 harmful species are recognized, cluster about roots and interfere with their activities, often with serious or even fatal results. "Spreading decline" in orchards and "worn-out soils" are often caused not by a lack of nutrients but by the activities of these tiny worms. Unless we are willing to abandon valuable farms or allow them to lie fallow for long periods of time, we must be able to recognize the causes of decline and the necessity to employ chemical treatments to reestablish productivity. Commercial nematology had its beginning just prior to World War II, when it was found that certain petroleum products would, when used before planting, cleanse Hawaiian pineapple fields of harmful nematodes at an acceptable cost. This method was so successful that its practice soon spread to the mainland and to a variety of other crops.

Weeds are the farmer's constant antagonists. They start to compete in the seedling row, with annual crops, at which time hand pulling may be the only solution. And although, later in the season, a few crops can outstrip the weeds, most of the crops are quickly overpowered unless continuous weed-control measures are employed. Our biggest agricultural-crop acreages in the United States are those of wheat, corn, and pastures, and these crops are grown under conditions that make hand weeding uneconomical. Selective chemical herbicides have made their greatest contribution with such crops by disposing of broad-leafed weeds. But there is a continuing search for something capable of the reverse effect, namely, of killing grassy weeds in such broad-leafed crops as sugar beets, cotton, and soybeans. It is now possible to destroy all weed seeds in the soil prior to planting; this is accomplished by the use of chemicals that quickly lose their toxicity or evaporate and thus make possible the subsequent planting of crops. At present, however, these chemicals are rather costly.

Another very valuable service performed by chemicals is that of defoliating and desiccating crop plants. The wide use of mechanical harvesters makes defoliation almost mandatory for cotton and certain other crops.

Many horticulturists have long suspected that plants, like people, require certain hormones, or vitamins, to help regulate and stimulate growth. A recent photograph, which aroused widespread interest, pictured a botanist looking up at a 10-foot cabbage plant, the result of treatment with a new growth stimulant known as gibberellin. We are not going to rush headlong into some Jack-and-the-beanstalk tomorrow-land, but it would be foolish not to run down such leads and see whether hormonal substances of this type cannot be used to advantage on crops and trees to speed up their rate of growth or to improve some desirable quality they possess. Some useful and remarkable accomplishments along this line have already been effected. There are, for example, chemical agents that are useful in getting cuttings to take root, in helping prevent apples and pears from dropping prematurely, in initiating flowering and fruiting cycles, in suppressing suckering in tobacco, and even in holding needles on Christmas trees for longer periods. It will take many years of patient work to determine what such chemicals can be made to do in relation to the over-all food supply, but the possibilities are there; the examples mentioned are merely an indication of things to come.

Veterinary science is already in a highly advanced stage. The veterinarian no longer waits for an animal to get down or out of production before attempting a cure. He has become a consultant on livestock nutrition and disease prevention, and his 250 million charges consume yearly over 60 million dollars worth of antibiotics, vitamins, coccidiostats, and anthelminthics to forestall their ills.

We take great satisfaction in our capacity to deal with disease in domestic animals. What about our sick plants? Here we still have a long way to go. To quote the eminent plant pathologist, James Horsfall, "Man has fought his animal pests with all he had but mostly he has fought his fungi with incantations and black magic." Nevertheless, considerable headway has been made in fighting plant sickness with foliage fungicides; and fungi and bacteria—in the form of rots, rusts, blights, smuts, wilts, mildews, leaf spots, yellows, declines, and diebacks—certainly represent some of the farmer's worst enemies. Losses due to fungi and bacteria are frequently higher than those due to insects, yet the poundage of fungicides now employed is scarcely a third that of the insecticides.

There are weapons against many fungus diseases; the older lime-sulfur and Bordeaux mixtures now have quite a few new complex synthetic organic allies. But we still have not achieved the phenomenal protective power that spelled such success for the insecticides; and economics still tend to limit the use of fungicides to the more expensive crops.

Plants, like animals, also suffer from virus-induced diseases, and we have yet to discover a single viricide that is practical for field application. The chemotherapy of virus diseases in both plants and animals is a fascinating study, one in which we can expect great research accomplishments. A few bacteria are also involved in plant disease, and as might be expected, it has been shown that these diseases can be controlled with antibiotics. The market for plant antibiotics is still small, but it is growing.

The rodents that live in our barns and houses eat the same kinds of foods that we eat and help to transmit diseases to us; unrestrained they could eat us out of house and home. But, here again, the synthetic organic chemist has come to our aid with some highly selective rodenticides. One of these is an anticoagulant that, when eaten in quantity by the rodent, causes death by internal bleeding.

These brief descriptions can no more than outline what chemicals are doing to protect plants from marauders and disease. Behind these achievements stands research, expenditures for which are lavish even by today's standards. In an industry where sales at the manufacturing level are somewhere between 250 and 300 million dollars per year, private research expenditures total about 30 million dollars per year. Much of this money goes into insuring against hazards to crops, animals, and man.

After a promising new agricultural chemical has been developed, one to two hundred thousand dollars may be spent to perfect formulae and to prove efficiency. Then comes perhaps a half million dollars in exhaustive testing to determine whether it can be used with safety to both farmer and consumer, and how to do so.

When a recommendation for the use of a given chemical is finally made by a state or Federal experiment station and followed by the grower, the consumer can be confident that any food product that has been so protected can be eaten with complete safety.

The important part played by modern industrial research in the discovery and development of new chemical materials is emphasized by a check of those listed in Hubert Martin's *Guide to the Chemicals Used in Crop Protection*. Before 1930 only 6 of the 43 chemicals developed were the result of industrial research; the remaining 37 came from tax-supported research institutions. In contrast, after 1930, of the 161 chemicals listed, 149 came from industrial research and 12 from tax-supported research institutions. The imagination and perseverance of the men and women who staff our agricultural chemical-industrial-research laboratories constitute our assurance of food in the future. The ever-increasing tempo of this research will keep the new plates full. A great deal has been accomplished in a relatively short time, but much more is yet to come.

Kenneth S. Adams has been chairman of the board and chief executive officer of Phillips Petroleum Company since 1951. Throughout his career, he has been actively interested in agriculture. His ranch at Foraker, Okla., is one of the leading centers of research in grassland farming.

Phillips Petroleum was one of the pioneers in the field of petroleum chemicals for agriculture and is a leading producer of farm fertilizers.

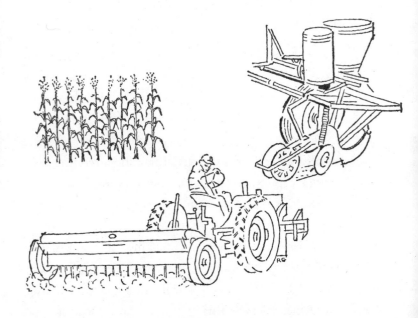

Making Land More Productive

Kenneth S. Adams

THE continued periods of famine and starvation in such great agricultural countries as China, India, and Russia, and the depleted lands and abandoned farms in some areas of our own country are facts that serve to remind us that the common practice of agriculture reduces the productive power of soils. Thus, one of the most important material problems of the United States is to maintain the fertility of her agricultural lands.

It is almost a universal rule that old land is less productive than new land. It has been said—many times in many ways—that if the art of agriculture has ruined land, the science of agriculture must restore and increase it. This process of restoration must be carried out while farmers are still prosperous; restoration requires substantial capital investments, and we must remember that we can expect no sound investments from poverty-stricken people.

Perhaps another way of looking at the problem would be to consider the plant-food demands of one of our basic crops. Corn is truly an all-American crop. The Americas gave this crop to world agriculture possibly in fair exchange for the many immigrant crops, including wheat and cotton, all of which contribute substantially to our economy. Although corn is not the crop that makes the greatest single cash contribution, the fact that it has over 600 uses and is grown almost everywhere in America makes it perhaps the crop of greatest prominence here. The United States Department of Agriculture estimated corn production for 1959 at 4.4 billion bushels. But when the corn harvesters completed their job, we knew that 1¾ million tons of elements representing plant food had been removed from our soils. The need of a program for the replacement of nitrogen, phosphate, potash, and other essential plant foods should be obvious.

The contribution of livestock and livestock products to farm income has steadily increased. For the past decade it has been the most important income factor in the welfare of farmers; livestock and its products currently contribute over 57 per cent of the total cash receipts from farm marketings. That our extensive grassland areas are the foundation of our basic livestock economy is a factor of which we all must be aware. Degree of efficiency in any given operation is an important consideration both in industry and in agriculture, and aside from the fact that quality grass is an economical source of livestock feed, the conversion efficiency or inefficiency of grain crops fed to livestock becomes one of these important considerations. It is roughly estimated that from pork about 24 per cent of the food value of grain is recovered for human consumption, from milk about 18 per cent, and from beef and mutton about 3.5 per cent. Roughages, therefore, must be given an increasing role in the economy of livestock feeding.

Another factor in maintaining fertility is the high efficiency of conversion of applied fertilizer materials in the first crop following application. Under many situations the uptake of nitrogen ranges from 40 to 70 per cent, of phosphate from 30 to 40 per cent, and of potash from 50 to 70 per cent. In case a yardstick is needed, consider the engine in your car or tractor with an average fuel-to-energy conversion factor of 10 to 15 per cent; then consider the tremendous role engines have played in the revolutionary advances on the farm. Practical-minded agricultural leaders and modern farmers have made great progress in developing and adapting new systems of farming to climate and other related factors that can and do affect crop production. As a nation we are favored with a wealth of basic resources, including such deposits as phosphate rock and potash salts, both containing essential plant foods; and energy fuels, including coal, shale, crude oil, and gas. But more important, we have a favorable climate in which to live and a wealth of aggressive and progressive farm and industry people who know how to work and grow together.

While it is true that the acreages of tillable and productive soils of the United States are likely to remain reasonably stable, and considering the checks and balances between urban encroachment and improvement of unused potential farmland, the adoption of new tools and skills and new crops and farm chemicals materially increase the efficiency and productiveness of today's modern farms. The inclusion of sod and green-manure crops in the crop sequence—a practice frequently overlooked—not only stabilizes the land against soil erosion, but builds up a deeper, more moisture-absorptive and more productive soil. The reclamation of poorly drained lands and the development of irrigation potentials of areas where rainfall and snowfall are not favorable also tend to expand the productive capacity of our farms.

As the modern farmer widens his horizon by farming deeper and more productively, one progressive step leads to another. The installation of an irrigation system, for instance, requires an additional capital investment, for it becomes important, then, that high-level production be undertaken. As the per-acre cost of production increases, inefficient yields of grain, grass, vegetables, beef, and other important products of the farm enterprise can no longer be tolerated by progressive farmers. In the future, quality of produce will also be stressed, and fringe benefits to farmers will result from high-quality beef, lamb, pork, and other livestock products. Higher levels and quality of protein in wheat, corn, and grazing crops, as well as of essential minerals in truck crops, will be the important goal of our farmers in the decades ahead.

Many factors play a role in the total economic impact of the modernization of farm business, factors that have helped to bring about what we all agree is a technological revolution in farm operations. Today's farm worker, for illustration, produces as much in one hour as he did in two hours in 1940 and in three hours in 1910. It would be a difficult task to list all of the innovations that have contributed to the high level of production of today's modern farm or ranch. We can agree, however, that the invention of the cotton gin, the gasoline tractor, and the mold-board plow, and the development of hybrids formed the bases for production spurts in the past. The development of the several families of antibiotics, insecticides, fungicides, and weedicides, and other farm chemicals have simplified the farmers' never-ending battle against plant and animal diseases, insects, and the other dangers against which he must wage continual warfare.

It is unfortunate that we tend to think of atomic energy in terms of instruments of warfare when its agricultural and industrial contributions are so obvious. For instance, its use as an economical source of radiation in the production of plant mutations, its application in food preservation, and its contribution to the study of medicinal drugs have been nothing short of miraculous. A number of companies have started "isotope farms" where such products are prepared for use by the research worker. The use of these products in diagnostic and therapy techniques in certain animal diseases and in screwworm control by irradiation of the male pupae represent only two of a number of new approaches to the problem of today's farmer. Never in the history of the world have agricultural innovations come into use at a faster pace than during the last two decades, and the time lag between invention and productive use has never been shorter.

The race toward the adoption of modern and more efficient farming methods presents a real challenge to the many supporting industries. The petroleum industry, for illustration, starting with improved fuels, lubricants, synthetic rubber, and heating oils for farms, has moved into plastics for irrigation pipes, chemicals for defoliants, insecticides, fungicides, and an even greater field, the combining of the hydrogen of natural gas with the nitrogen of the air to produce fertilizer for expanded crop production.

Use of plant foods is increasing rapidly. During

1935-1936 about 1⅓ million tons of primary plant foods—nitrogen, available phosphate, and potash—were sold. By 1957-1958 this figure had reached over 6½ million tons, or nearly five times the 1935-1936 sale. Sale of fertilizer materials and mixtures, in which the farmer obtains these plant foods, amounted to more than 22½ million tons in 1957-1958; and when other soil amendments, such as ground limestone, other liming materials, and gypsum, are included, this figure is increased to well over 40 million tons.

Although cropland has steadily diminished in the United States since 1936 and farm manpower has dropped at even a greater rate, production on American farms has continued year after year to increase. As an ally to the mechanization of farming, plant foods —including the all-important nitrogen—have played a highly important part.

In 1898, Sir William Crookes, a famous English chemist, discussed the problem of crop production in an address before the British Association for the Advancement of Science. He first pointed to the world's growing population and its increasing need for wheat and other food crops. Crookes then described his own discovery, a means by which the inert nitrogen gas of the atmosphere could be made to combine with the oxygen in the atmosphere by being passed through the intense heat of an electric arc. By adding water this oxide became nitric acid, which could be neutralized by sodium carbonate to produce a synthetic nitrate of soda. All that was needed to make this a practical method was a cheap source of electric energy, and Crookes observed that Niagara Falls represented a place where it could be produced. The chemical industry, always alert to new possibilities, immediately set out to try to develop this process on a factory scale. In 1905 the first such nitrogen-fixing factory was put into operation in Norway; it produced nitrate of lime, using limestone as a neutralizing agent instead of sodium carbonate.

As other methods of nitrogen fixation began to be studied, Fritz Haber of Germany found that, by the joint use of high pressure and temperatures, he could join atmospheric nitrogen with hydrogen gas to produce ammonia; in 1913 a factory employing this process was put into operation in Germany. Since that time many improvements have been made in what is now known as the Haber-Bosch method, modifications of which are now widely employed the earth over.

At the outbreak of World War II, we were caught in the dilemma of having not only to feed and clothe ourselves but our allies as well, even though imports of nitrogen and potash were sharply curtailed. Moreover, the need for explosives made from nitrogen products mounted at a staggering rate. With assistance from our government and the full cooperation of American industry, a number of strategically placed anhydrous ammonia plants were built. Through the magic of chemistry, physics, and related sciences, and a good sprinkling of engineering "know-how," a whole family of nitrogen products, such as ammonium nitrate, ammonium sulfate, and urea, was created. The raw materials used in this process consisted first of the air about us. With three-fourths of its content in the form of the elusive element nitrogen and the availability of rich sources of petroleum materials, including natural gas and coal, as a supply of hydrogen, American industry was well on its way to meeting the primary emergency and opening new horizons for farm production as well.

Initially, the most urgent needs, of course, were for explosives, for related industrial demands, and for nitrogen fertilizers sorely needed by the farmers to increase yields of food, feed, and fiber. The demand was so great that the full resources of varied American industries were called upon to double and treble production facilities. Not least of the groups responding was the petroleum industry. A dozen or more members of the industry—some big, some relatively small, but all able and earnest—leaned to the task, and today we have nearly 60 basic nitrogen plants, well placed to serve the needs of America's great agricultural food factory. Not only do we have nitrogen in varied forms to suit the needs of the fertilizer manufacturer and distributor, but we have compounds that are useful as animal feeds, refrigerants, chemicals, plastics, propellants, and synthetics, and numerous other valuable products as well. Thus, with either natural gas, coal, by-product hydrogen, or other hydrogen-bearing materials, plus the nitrogen naturally occurring in the air—and through the knowledge of today's scientists—we continue to expand nitrogen products for tomorrow's people.

The fertilizer industry as a whole has done a magnificent job of, first, assembling the basic plant foods —including products designed for special soil conditions—and secondary and trace minerals; and second, manufacturing compounds to meet unusual circumstances, thus keeping pace with the soil scientist. As a measure of the efficiency of American farms, the production of the major storable crops .has been maintained despite acreage allotments, marketing quotas, and related control measures.

Fortunately, there is virtually no limit to the supplies of raw materials out of which soil amendments can be produced. Limestone deposits are far greater than will ever be required in the foreseeable future. Nitrogen supplies, totaling some 35,000 tons in the air over every acre of land, are inexhaustible. Next to Morocco, the United States has the world's largest deposits of high-grade phosphate rock, estimated at over 13 billion tons. Although our potash reserves, contained for the most part in deep-down deposits in an area around Carlsbad, New Mexico, are estimated at only 400 million tons, tremendous additional tonnages of potash salts, believed to be greater than the 20 billion tons in the famous Stassfurt deposits in Germany, were recently discovered in the Canadian province of Saskatchewan.

The American fertilizer industry is doing an impressive job of fixing nitrogen, and of mining, processing, and assembling all the mineral plant foods, including the secondary and trace elements, that are required for crop production. It has assembled a manpower pool whose research and technological knowledge can be depended on to keep farmers supplied with an abundance of all the needed plant foods. It is also developing new fertilizer materials designed to meet the particular requirements for the several soils, climates, and crops, and for the intensity of production required.

Fertilizers are now being produced in more concentrated forms, which means much more plant food in every ton and a substantial saving in freight and handling costs. Anhydrous ammonia gas, compressed to liquid form, is being applied on a large scale directly into the soil. Liquid nitrogen fertilizers, liquid phosphoric acid, ammonium phosphate, and complete fertilizers are now available in quantity. Solid fertilizers are being produced in granular forms that flow freely from the distributor. In many areas farmers buy their fertilizers on the basis of ease of delivery to the field and application to the land.

In the opinion of many economists, the market for quality farm products will, in the foreseeable future, be greatly expanded. In the United States nearly 50 million new customers have been added since 1930, and by 1975 this figure is expected to increase by an estimated 65 million. In addition to this continuous growth in our domestic market, the food needs of rapidly increasing populations throughout the world brings fresh impetus to the development and expansion of foreign markets.

In the meantime, productivity of agriculture is likely to continue to rise. Increased use of fertilizers, irrigation developments, and other sound management practices will continue to be adopted, with the result that the years ahead will see even greater records in farm production. The technological revolution in agriculture has just begun on the farms of America.

A giant's stride has been made from our former reliance on the sumbiotic fixation of nitrogen by legume plants to our present reliance on synthetic ammonia plants as a basic source of nitrogen for America's farms. There is no quarrel with the increased use of green-manure crops, including legumes in the areas where adequate precipitation or irrigation water is present, where their use is in conjunction with live-stock projects and where soil conditioning is a problem. However, the growing of legumes as a prime source of nitrogen becomes a luxury that the modern farmer can hardly afford. The fertilizer industry has assembled a manpower pool with technical know-how in processing and distributing, one sufficient to guarantee a reserve storehouse of nitrogen, phosphate, potash, and other plant-food requirements for the future. The income of the farmer, the quality of his crops, and the guarantee of abundant yields will be assured for tomorrow. They will serve notice to the world that the ingenuity and capacity of America's team—industry and agriculture—is unbounded.

The national potential for meeting the agricultural needs for nitrogen, phosphate, and potash in the future is most encouraging. Able industrial organizations, including the National Plant Food Institute, have worked closely with the many state experiment stations and the United States Department of Agriculture on a detailed study of the plant-food potential of the several states. One state, famed for its corn production, is today using only 12 per cent of its potential nitrogen need. In the event the factors of education, information, and economics could be applied to the problem and the use of nitrogen increased to match the potential need, this one state alone could use a fourth of the present national production of nitrogen earmarked for agriculture. Significant, too, is the fact that eight grain-belt states have a potential plant-food nitrogen need equal to America's present scheduled production.

It can be said with considerable emphasis and satisfaction that the chemical industry, and the petroleum group in particular, can meet the challenge of added production and distribution facilities for the major plant-food and industrial needs for tomorrow's people.

Robert S. Stevenson has been president of Allis-Chalmers Manufacturing Company since 1955 and is a past president of the Farm Equipment Institute. A native of the state of Washington and a graduate of Washington State College, he joined Allis-Chalmers in 1933.

Allis-Chalmers has pioneered many advances and developments in farm mechanization and today is one of the leading companies in the field of farm machinery and equipment.

Increasing Productivity by
Power Farming

Robert S. Stevenson

THE plate of food you expect without question for your next meal is your share of a huge power-farming plateful from which we all eat. We take our abundance for granted, yet the same 450 to 500 million cropland acres in the United States that are feeding 180 million of us today were, as late as 1940, feeding less than 132 million people. And in 1975

99

substantially these same acres will be called on to feed
some 245 million of us. Today's surpluses, which loom
so large in political headlines and market economics,
are estimated by some as no more than 6 per cent above
actual use, but by 1975, our needs will require 35 to 40
per cent more than we produce today.

Contrary to what many people believe, keeping pace
with our growing dinner-table demand will *not* require a farming miracle. It will simply call for the
expansion of our power farming and the continuation
of other modern trends already started. Let me illus-
trate. In 1940, mechanical and electrical horsepower
on American farms together totaled less than ½ horsepower per acre for our nearly constant 475 million
acres of cropland. Today, 20 years later, that horsepower figure has more than doubled: we are now
applying more than 1 full horsepower per cropland
acre. It would thus seem safe to assume that, if needed,
by 1975 we could similarly double the horsepower used
today. In other words, in 1975 we quite possibly may
average 2 horsepower in power-farming equipment—
tractors, stationary engines, self-propelled machines,
trucks, cars, and electric motors—for every cropland
acre.

In intensive farming areas, we have already demonstrated what we can expect in production with such an input of power coupled to modern methods. In the market crop area of New Jersey, for example, some growers are already applying 2½ horsepower per acre. To ask how far we will finally go in the application of horsepower to cropland is like asking an oilman how deep he will drill for oil. The amount of horsepower that will be used on farms, like drilling depth in the oilfields, depends on needs. Leaders in both of these great industries share the same philosophy that, whatever the requirement, they have the men and machines to find an answer to it.

Today there are 4½ million tractors of all sizes in use on farms. How many will our farmers be operating in 1975? The actual number will depend on the size and type of machines preferred in the years ahead; but in terms of today's three-plow tractors, by 1975 we can anticipate 2¼ million additional tractors on United States farms. This estimate is based on a 2-horsepower per acre need, with tractors supplying, as they do today, at least a fourth of that power. For the farm-equipment industry this increase will mean not only much new business but a sturdy growth of the annual replacement market. Since the farmer of the future, being a businessman, can be expected to use his tractor for as many hours of production work as possible in order to realize a maximum return from his investment, tractors will be used harder and for more jobs and more hours each year. The sale of tractors in 1959 did not keep pace with the necessity for replacements, so, as a growing population makes its needs felt, the industry must, in addition to required expansion, make up this deficit.

Another way to look at food for the future is in terms of the farm horsepower available to feed each consuming person. Back in 1940, only 1.6 horsepower was helping the nation's farmers feed each consumer; the rest of the work load was carried on human backs or by horses and mules. In 1950, this figure was 2.5 horsepower. Based on the projected population and total farming horsepower needed in 1975, just under 4 farming horsepower for each consumer would appear ample to wrest the required food from the same acres we use now.

Farm horsepower per cropland acre and farm horsepower per consumer, together give us a real measure of power farming in the future. They also explain why, in food production history, farm power and food abundance have been so consistently linked together. In older civilizations, whether free or slave, any attempt to increase production meant putting more people and animals to work on the land, and such all-out efforts for more food defeated themselves because the expected increase was consumed by the extra people and animals before it left the farmland where it was grown. The inescapable conclusion is this: when mechanical horsepower is added to available acres, the food produced is increased, *but the increase is not eaten up before it leaves the farm.* In other words, tractors, trucks, engines, and electric motors do not consume the extra food they help produce.

Now, let us look at the other side of the power-farming picture. While current machines, and those yet to be developed, are providing power to assist in the widespread application of each new agronomic advance, what happens to the farm itself? What happens to the people who are a part of this great agricultural industry?

Let us start with that old tradition, the family farm. Here we are thinking of an operation that will yield enough farm produce to provide a satisfactory living for the particular family involved and yet to be handled largely without dependence on outside help. Today, thousands of farmers are proving that a family operation can grow and change to fit new business necessities. Like retailers, farmers are learning fast to provide the homemaker with what she wants, rather than expect her to accept what sentiment and tradition might dictate. It may be fun to read about grandpa's apple barrel, but what we do is buy our fruit orchard-packed in pliofilm. Yesterday's smokehouse of fat hams may stimulate a certain nostalgia, but those hams lack the appeal of today's supermarket counterpart from meat-type hogs. Progressive farm families are staying on top of such trends by specialization; the fruit farmer, dairyman, vegetable producer, broiler grower, and turkey raiser are all becoming single-line specialists.

And as the family farm specializes, it too can afford to mechanize its operations completely. In addition to the greater horsepower per acre already mentioned, this specialized mechanization also necessitates tractors and related machines tailored to specific requirements for much greater efficiency. The general diversified farmer of today with 15 or 20 dairy cows may use a milking machine and carry his herd during much of the year on 25 to 40 acres of pasture. But if this same man becomes a specialized dairyman, he can afford to use a forage harvester and bring his pasture grasses fresh to the cattle each day. Such a program, coupled with improved pasture management, can double the feed production of his pastureland, permitting a herd of 40 or even 50 cows. And with this number the dairyman can go the rest of the way. His individual-unit milking machine will be replaced by a pipeline system in a milking parlor. His old milk cans will be discarded in favor of a bulk tank. Horsepower, instead of human muscle, will do most of the work. Even washing the pipeline and milking units becomes a power operation.

No discussion of this kind would be complete without a forward look at the farm tractor itself. Here, as before, the best yardstick of the future would seem to be the progress made up to the present. Back in 1921, as farm tractors began to make a name for themselves, one of the more efficient three-plow models was rated at 30 horsepower on the belt and 20 horsepower on the drawbar. To obtain this power an engine with 461 cubic inches of cylinder displacement was required. Twenty years later, the descendant of this early model had 34 horsepower on the belt and 28 horsepower on the drawbar, and it rolled on rubber tires. Although horsepower had gone up, engine size had gone down to 301 cubic inches. Maximum pull, as recorded in the Nebraska Tractor Tests, was 2,593 pounds. Today, the

latest type three-plow tractor in the same line has 35
belt horsepower, with 32 on the drawbar, and a maximum pull of 4,847 pounds. And it takes only 149 cubic
inches of cylinder displacement in the engine to do the
job. Since 1941, engine power per cubic inch has
doubled, and drawbar pull has gone up 86 per cent.
At the same time, fuel economy has been improved by
as much as 24 per cent.

In addition to offering this greater efficiency, some
tractors today also use automatic weight transfer to
"nail down" the extra drawbar pull for useful field
work. With such a system, tractor and implements become truly a team. The tractor is no longer just a
source of power with modified horse-type units trailed
behind. Instead, tractor and implements have been
combined into one highly specialized unit, in effect a
roving machine tool for working the soil, planting the
crop, controlling the weeds, and bringing in the harvest.

These modern-farming requirements have been responsible for the evolution of the tractor into a highly
complex machine. Each year has added to the number
of gear speeds, the power control system, and the hy-
draulics desired for mounted and drawn equipment.
And behind each change has been a farm need to in-

crease the application of power—to handle more jobs and to handle them faster and to provide greater comfort and convenience for the operator.

In the future, even greater specialization and efficiency may be expected. This is what the farmer wants, and he has demonstrated his willingness to make the extra investment required. Farm-equipment dealerships, too, will continue their tendency to develop more complete service stations for the power farmer. By 1975, a large percentage of the dealers will need to be application engineers, giving their customers skilled guidance in farm-equipment selection and use. The dealers of tomorrow—even more than those of today—will spend much of their time in the country, becoming intimately acquainted with the needs of each specialized farming operation. Their service, farm by farm, will be nearly as important to crop production as the telephone service of today is to communication.

The entire history of power farming is a record of flexible service, of supplying each agricultural area with the kind of power and tools it needs in each particular decade of progress. In 1975 farm power will be the power that agriculture, on one hand, and the consuming public, on the other, desire.

*Robert E. Wilson is a former board chairman
and chief executive officer of Standard Oil
Company (Indiana). He was trained as a
chemical engineer and served on the faculty of
the Massachusetts Institute of Technology before
joining Standard Oil in 1922. Dr. Wilson has
served on many government and industry
committees, and for many years was chairman
of the Research Committee of the American
Petroleum Institute board of directors.
He is a member of the United States
Atomic Energy Commission.*

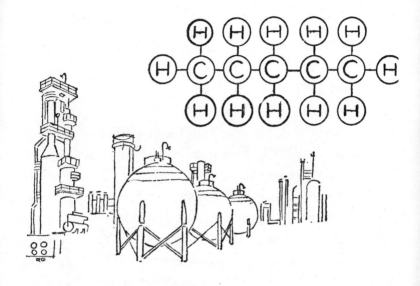

Energy in Abundance

Robert E. Wilson

AS he faces his task of feeding 240 million people in 1975, the American farmer will first want to know if he is going to have land enough to do the job. A quick review shows that he will. Even without increasing the number of acres now under cultivation, in 1975 the United States will have, per person, twice as much cropland as western Europe now has, and ten times as much as Japan. With respect to land, we seem to be well off.

Another important question is, will we have enough fuel to run our tractors and other farm machines in 1975? The answer is an unqualified yes. No matter how great the progress in tractors and other farm equipment, the petroleum industry can guarantee ample supplies of both fuels and lubricants well beyond 1975. Yet adequate supply is only part of the story for farmers. Makers of equipment and providers of energy will have to plan carefully if the foods of the future are to be supplied at reasonable costs. The real job of the oil industry is to determine the best and most economical ways of meeting farmers' needs, a job far more complex than is the simple statement of ability.

Power farming is already saving a tremendous amount of human labor and with remarkable production results. The average farm worker today produces food and fiber for three times as many people as he did in 1910. His efficiency has been increased 200 per cent. His tractors do not eat oats, hay, and other crop products, and he has better strains of plants and livestock, with better chemicals to protect them from pests and diseases. But most important of all he has more and better farm machinery, which enables him to work more land and do a greater variety of farm jobs in the time available.

The improvements the farmer enjoys would not have been practical, however, had farm machinery continued to burn the coal and wood used by the old-fashioned threshing machine. To a great extent his more efficient equipment has been made possible by the availability of low-cost liquid fuels derived from petroleum. Today the average farmer spends only about $300 a year for his highly efficient modern fuels. For that amount plus a reasonable expenditure for his machines, he has acquired the equivalent in work of at least two additional farmers and several teams of horses. He is thus not likely to give up his machines unless the cost of energy to run them gets entirely out of hand. Let us see what the prospects are.

Dire predictions that we are running out of oil have been heard for more than 60 years. In 1892 the United States Bureau of Mines estimated that the country's *total* potential production would be no more than 5.7 billion barrels. That, however, was before geophysicists and other scientists were put to work on exploration for sources of oil and its production. Despite repeated examples of pessimism on the part of government estimators, these scientists and engineers have already enabled the industry to produce a total of 60 billion barrels. In addition, the presently proven oil reserves total more than 32 billion barrels, and we fully expect to go on finding new oil fields. We are also continually finding better ways of getting the oil out of the ground. Where once only about 20 per cent of the oil could be wrested from the porous rocks in which it occurs, as much as 70 per cent can now be obtained. Possibly 100 billion barrels more could be recovered from oil fields by use of such modern techniques as gas pressuring, water drives, rock splitting by hydraulic pressure, and other methods that are still in the experimental stage.

Each barrel of oil produced, however, means that there is one less barrel to be discovered. Since it is not logical to assume that we can go on forever finding new fields, as crude oil becomes more expensive to find and produce, other competitive sources will have to be exploited. The most promising is oil shale. On the basis of the United States Geological Survey's recently revised estimate of our resources of high-grade shale, the deposits in Colorado alone would, at the present rate of consumption of liquid fuels, supply the country's needs for over 300 years!

Crude shale oil can be produced even now for slightly less than the cost of petroleum. Unfortunately, it is not as good a starting material for making oil products because it is heavy and tarry and contains large quantities of impurities. The cost of gasoline made from it would be about 30 per cent more than at present. Research will no doubt lead to better ways of mining and processing and thus lower costs. In any event, the fact of the country's large deposits of oil shale places a ceiling on the future price of liquid fuels.

We also know how to make gasoline from coal, and reserves of coal in the United States are far larger than reserves of petroleum. In other parts of the world gasoline has already been made commercially from coal by several different processes.

Tar sands, too, furnish a source of oil. At present these tar sands are hard to process, but a new method of underground burning may eventually make it easier to recover the oil from the sands.

So even if petroleum should not be able to carry the whole burden, one or another of these sources will undoubtedly provide plenty of liquid fuel for the farmer of 1975, but even if this were not so, the farmer has still other potential sources of fuel. If it became necessary, he could grow his own fuels just as he "grew" them for his horses in earlier days. Corn and other farm products can be turned into alcohol and utilized in this form as fuel. The present trend, however, is just the reverse: for economic reasons there has been a growing tendency to convert fuels to alcohol rather than alcohol to fuels. For example, five years ago about half the country's industrial alcohol came from molasses and half from petroleum, but today the proportion of alcohol that comes from molasses has dropped to about 10 per cent. As for the use of corn, even at a price of $1.32 a bushel, a gallon of alcohol would cost 68 cents, or more than six times the present refinery price of gasoline, and the energy content of such alcohol is only 62 per cent as high as that of gasoline. Possibly alcohol could also be made from agricultural wastes, where the gathering cost of the wastes would be borne by the main food or fiber product. But no matter what the source, in 1975 alcohol will still be too costly to be used as a motor fuel.

We are probably likewise safe in saying that atomic energy will not be used to drive farm tractors and other equipment in 1975; even if it should become as cheap as liquid fuels for some purposes, it would be far too inconvenient and dangerous for use on farm equipment.

The future may see marked changes, however, in the power plant; we hear about gas turbines, free-piston engines, fuel-injection engines, and so on. But in this area predictions are best left to the equipment makers.

Suffice it to note here that all these engines will require liquid fuels, preferably of the hydrocarbon type.

There is also a possibility that new devices may eventually supersede the heat engine. As the result of many years of research, heat engines are now almost as efficient as they are likely to become. The thermal efficiency of the rugged mobile engines needed for tractors and trucks will probably never rise much above an average of 30 per cent. This relatively low efficiency is due, of course, to the laws of thermodynamics. Any heat engine is bound to waste a large part of the energy put into it, and although ways can be found to reduce this waste, they tend to cost more than the energy saved is worth.

Electrolytic cells, however, are not handicapped by this thermodynamic problem. Already, experimental cells are turning fuel energy from hydrogen into work at efficiencies reported to be around 70 per cent. Making hydrogen from coal or petroleum is, of course, expensive, but there is a possibility that cells can be developed that would operate on hydrocarbons directly. The type of machine may change, but it seems more than likely that the farmer, the farm machinery industry, and the oil industry will continue their present partnership.

Petroleum does more, of course, than supply energy. It also supplies lubricating oils, used not only for lubricating purposes but also as a base for greases. And petroleum contains a surplus of these oils. To supply the country's needs, we now use much less than half of the lube fraction obtained in our refineries. The rest is cracked to gasoline. So, even when our supply of crude oil dwindles, petroleum will still be able to furnish us with sufficient lubricants.

In the distant future, when perhaps our liquid fuels are being made from shale or coal, a number of processes will make possible the production of synthetic lube oils. As far back as 1932, normal olefins were being polymerized to make a special high-quality oil. It was a better oil than the engines of the day required, but it could not be sold for less than 75 cents a quart. If a future need arises, however, that project could be revived to supply lubricating oil for farm machinery.

Chemical companies, too, have ventured into the field of synthetic lubricants, some with a degree of success. Synthetic lubes are now being sold for special purposes. One company tried to market a synthetic motor oil of the type of compounds known to chemists as polyglycols, which, although it was not quite able to capture the motorist's business, did find some industrial uses.

The farmers of 1975 will have no trouble getting lubricating oil in the quantities they will need. The important question is what kinds they will want. Today there seems to be a growing demand for special products, such as, for example, hydraulic oils, with extreme-pressure additives, for use in torque amplifiers. The farmer and the farm-machinery manufacturers would be well advised to move in the direction of multi-purpose lubricants whereby the same fuels, oils, and greases can be used in car, truck, and tractor. The farmer, himself, has moved toward some standardization in the use of fuels; for example, he has rejected the kerosene tractor in favor of the more useful and convenient gasoline type. A similar trend in respect to lubricants would be equally advantageous to him. Despite the increasing severity of modern service, additives and other advances have made oils and greases far more versatile than they used to be, and a relatively small list of products can now satisfy almost all lubricant needs. Whatever the products of such a list turn out to be, the farmer can be assured that the oil industry will be able to furnish them to him.

The farmer's tractor, driven by petroleum energy and

lubricated by petroleum oils and greases, runs on tires that, too, tend more and more to be based on petroleum. The chief raw materials for synthetic rubber are butylene, butadiene, styrene, and similar hydrocarbons, all of which can be readily made from crude oil. Here again there is no danger of a shortage. The rubber industry is a large and important one; yet the annual consumption of rubber in the United States, both natural and synthetic, amounts to less than half of 1 per cent of the country's annual production of petroleum. Many other modern needs, too, can be satisfied entirely from petroleum without endangering the supply that other uses of petroleum require.

Few farm products can reach their market without experiencing, at some point, travel on an asphalt road. In rural areas asphalt roads outnumber those made of concrete by 7 to 1, and for the wider highways, the ratio is 4 to 1. The superhighways in New Jersey, Maine, and Oklahoma are all asphalt, but even a concrete highway uses asphalt in expansion joints and the replacement of worn surfaces.

In the many areas where water is scarce, any increase in cropland will require increased use of irrigation, and one of the biggest problems is how to get irrigation water to growing plants without undue waste. By using asphalt, along with other petroleum based materials, to line irrigation ditches, both water losses and costs of irrigation are reduced.

The farmer also requires a great deal of roofing asphalt and tar paper. All these and other uses make the future supply of asphalt a matter for our attention. Here the picture is even brighter, if possible, than it is with respect to the other petroleum products. Heavy, asphaltic crudes, along with the other asphaltic deposits, are plentiful. But much more asphalt could be made by the oil industry than is now being made. Shale oil is also a possible raw material. One fact is sure: we can continue to criss-cross the country with smooth black hydrocarbon highways and still have plenty of asphalt to meet other needs.

Scientific research is steadily giving us new ways of turning petroleum into more useful materials. Scientists can make big molecules out of little ones and little ones out of big ones and can tailor all of them into the shapes best suited for each of many special uses.

The farmer of 1975 need not worry about supplies of all the petroleum-derived products he will require. One general and important fact in this whole question of future needs is that our real future resource is not any substance; it is not so many barrels of oil in the ground or even the nuclei of so many atoms that are suitable for fission or fusion. The answers to our future needs will be found in science and technology. There is great diversity in science. Perhaps our energy problem will be solved by a scientist now studying electronic configurations in silicon, or some other subject that seems to have nothing to do with today's practical uses of energy. But if we have alert scientists and engineers, and give them freedom to explore and develop, and if we retain the incentives for industry to keep them at work, there will be no shortage of any product that people really want and need. Ways of meeting our long-range needs are clearly in sight, but we must find not merely a way to solve a problem, we must find the best way. Countries, as well as companies and industries, are working in competition one with the other to achieve this. Right now the goal of considerable petroleum research is higher octane numbers, to permit more efficient use of the fuel supply. This problem will gradually give way to others, but success in reaching any goal, whatever it may be, requires research. Inevitable and vital progress demands the knowledge and understanding that become available through research.

We must make sure we have a good supply of the vital raw materials. We must keep intact the existing incentives, such as the depletion deduction, which makes it worthwhile to hunt for petroleum on the American continent; for, although shale or coal can supply our needs in the long run, it would take years to convert refineries to their use. A large part of our research must be done within independent companies rather than by the government. And most important of all, we must attract able young people into science and engineering. They will do the job of making fuels, lubricants, power-farming equipment, and all else needed by farmers in 1975 and in the centuries ahead.

Philip D. Reed was, before his retirement, chairman of the board of General Electric Company for 19 years. A native of Milwaukee, he received a degree in electrical engineering from the University of Wisconsin and a law degree from Fordham University. During World War II, Mr. Reed served as chief of the Bureau of Industries of the War Production Board.

As a leading manufacturer of electrical equipment, General Electric has for many years pioneered in the research and application of electricity to agriculture.

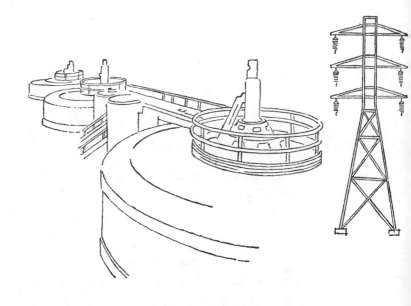

Electricity and
the Business of Farming

Philip D. Reed

THE United States of America, or the economic status enjoyed by its people, has no parallel in history. With only 7 per cent of the world's population, we produce 40 per cent of the world's goods; with only 6 per cent of the land area on our mainland we produce 15 per cent of the world's food calories. For our consumption American industry provides not only a tremendous quantity but also a wide variety and great diversity of goods and services. And American agriculture enables us to have a diet that is not only adequate in calories but abundant in appetizing and nutritious animal products.

The standard of living of a people can be measured in two ways. What the average family can buy with what it earns in a normal work week—which includes not only such basic items as food, clothing, housing, but also the nonessential goods and services that contribute so much to our happiness and well-being—provides one measure. It can also be measured by the length of the normal work week, or, to put it the other way round, by the amount of leisure time available to the average family for physical, cultural, and spiritual enjoyment.

A close relationship exists between the per capita energy utilization of a country and its national income, living standards, and output. Only by lengthening man's arm and multiplying his power to produce, by increasing his output per day and week, can we have *both* more goods and more leisure. The push-button power available to the industrial worker in this country has grown so steadily since the turn of the century that today the average manufacturing worker uses more than 20,000 kilowatt-hours of electrical energy a year to help him turn out his product. In agriculture, the power machines used in farm operations—tractors, stationary engines, self-propelled machines, trucks, automobiles, and electric motors—now represent an estimated total of at least 1 horsepower for every cropland acre. The average per capita expenditure of such energy in the United States is six times that in the world as a whole.

The availability of this abundant energy in useful form has revolutionized American industry and agriculture. In factories, the application of electric power, with its advantages of flexibility, cleanliness, and control, has erased many of the adverse effects that came with the steam engine and has made possible the good working conditions, high productivity, and excellent wages of today. In agriculture, the substitution of mechanical and electric power for animal and human muscle power has increased productivity per man; while the application of improved fertilizers and insecticides, better varieties of plants and animals, and improved soil and water conservation practices have markedly increased productivity per acre.

The revolution in agriculture has been one of the most profound and significant of any segment of our economy. Output per man-hour has almost doubled since 1940, and, in spite of the fact that there are 10 million fewer people living on farms, the farmer is taking care of the food and fiber requirements of 45 million more people, the increase in our population during that period. To put it another way, each farm worker in the United States is now supplying food for himself and 18 other people in this country, plus 2 persons abroad. By contrast, in 1940 each farm worker supplied himself and 10 others, but at the beginning of the century he supplied a total of only 7 people. In Soviet Russia today, it apparently takes 2 workers on farms to supply themselves and 3 other persons with food and clothing.

In America, it was the rural sections that felt last, although not least, the revolutionary impact of electric light and power. There are still many adult farm-born Americans who can remember carrying water and cleaning the chimneys of kerosene lamps. As one writer remarked, "Unless you have lived by lamplight or fired a washpot in the back yard, you'll never know what electricity really means."

The first electric power plant, built by Thomas A. Edison in 1882, generated direct current. Since this low-voltage current could be transmitted only a few miles, the power plants were located in cities close to their customers. By about 1900, technological advance had produced a practical steam turbine, transformer, and alternating-current transmission. In the following two decades, larger, more efficient generating stations were built and connected by transformers and transmission lines to load centers.

During this early period, some efforts were made to apply electricity to farm operations. Around the turn of the century, some West Coast electric utilities built farm lines for irrigation purposes. In 1908, the General Electric Company hired two college graduates with degrees in agriculture and electrical engineering and sent them out with various types of electrical apparatus and testing equipment to perform various farm operations electrically and determine the feasibility of such applications. This led, in 1911, to the publication of *Electricity on the Farm,* perhaps the first book on the subject.

By 1920, electric utility companies had built a vast network of transmission lines that provided 24-hour electric service to virtually every city and village in the United States; and the steam turbine had been developed to a point where the cost of producing electricity was greatly reduced. These developments, along with improvements in the methods of distributing electricity to farms, made it possible for the first time to supply adequate electric power at low price to farms distant from urban centers.

In 1921, the National Electric Light Association organized a rural electric service committee to see how electricity could be applied in farming. Rural electrification involved more than merely building lines along the highways; if electricity was to be of maximum usefulness to the farmer, new farm machinery had to be developed and new methods of farming evolved. To assist in this development, a joint committee of national scope was set up; it included representatives of the American Farm Bureau Federation, the National Grange, the American Society of Agricultural Engineers, the United States Department of Agriculture, the electrical industry, and others. This cooperative organization, known as the Committee on the Relation of Electricity to Agriculture, was organized in 1923 to promote research and development work at universities and among manufacturers and to publish and distribute material on the applications of electricity to the farm. Industry advertising, motion pictures, and radio programs (such as WGY's "Farm Forum," inaugurated in 1925) played important roles in this work. The result was that, by 1928, electric utilities were extending service to agriculture at the rate of more than 100,000 farms a year.

The economic depression of the early 1930s halted this expansion temporarily, but by 1935 industry was able to resume its rural electrification program. In the same year the Rural Electrification Administration (REA) was organized by the Federal government, and through its loans to newly organized REA cooperatives it became an important factor in making the use of electricity possible for farm operations. In recent years, the application of electricity to farm operations has kept pace with the growth of the electrical industry itself, doubling every 10 years. Today, more than 95 per cent of the farms in the United States are electrified, and these 4.5 million farms are using more than 22 billion kilowatt-hours of electricity a year.

What of the future? With 95 per cent of all American farms electrified and virtually 100 per cent of the productive farms already connected, it may seem strange to predict a tremendous expansion for rural electrification. But new uses for electricity continue to emerge in direct proportion to the manpower and dollars that industry is spending on research and development. In terms of the applications of electric

power that could be profitably made today, the average
farm is, in truth, only about 25 per cent electrified.

The familiar projections of population shift and
growth indicate that by 1975 farmers in the United
States must produce enough food to meet the needs of
240 million people in this country alone. For the past
20 years, 110,000 farms have on the average disappeared
each year. If this continues, by 1975 less than 3.5 million farms will remain and there will be only 15 million people living on them. It will be these 15 million
people who will have the heavy responsibility of meeting the food and fiber needs of almost a quarter of a
billion people. To accomplish this, Edison Electric
Institute has estimated that, by 1975, American farmers
will need the help of twice as much electricity and the
appliances and equipment by which it can be utilized,
or, in other words, an average of 10,000 kilowatt-hours
per farm per year.

How will this electrical energy be used? Some future
uses can already be predicted. By 1975, we can expect
the up-to-date dairy farmer to have, in addition to his
automatic watering system, his well-lighted barn and
his milking machine, complete equipment for his other
undertakings. This equipment will include such things
as pipeline milking direct from the cow to the bulk

milk cooler; silo unloaders automatically controlled to deliver silage direct from the silo to the feed barn; and time switches to start up the barn cleaner and get the job done before the farmer gets up to do the milking. Cows will be eating better-quality hay, cut at its best stage of maturity and barn-cured. Home-grown grain, dried with the farmer's crop dryer, will be ground, mixed, and piped directly to the cows to take care of their individual grain requirements that have been electronically computed by a university or an industry. And electricity will have taken over age-old chores. The average dairy farmer now lifts, carries, or pushes 30 to 40 tons of material per cow per year. Electricity will perform these tasks for less than a nickel a day. Instead of caring for 20 cows a day the average dairy farmer will be taking care of 40 high-milk producers, thus, in effect, doubling his labor income.

By 1975, the average commercial poultry farmer will be caring for layers at the rate of at least 10,000 per man, with all the basic operations—watering, feeding, ventilating, air-conditioning, cleaning—electrified. Automatic egg handling will have become common practice: the egg will be automatically removed from the nest, graded, and delivered directly to the cooling room, and all within a few minutes after the egg is laid. Broiler production will have passed the billion and a half mark, with individual producers marketing 150,000 or more broilers per man per year. And electricity will be doing the watering, feeding, ventilating, lighting, and supplying of radiant energy for automatic brooding. From birth to marketing, each chick in 1975 will use nearly 1 kilowatt-hour of electricity.

Automatic feed handling, including the grinding, mixing, and delivering of feed direct from storage to feed bunk, will reduce labor for all cattle-feeding operations. Already, individual operators are feeding from 500 to 1,000 steers or more in dry lots by pushing a few buttons; and they could replace these buttons with time switches and have automatic controls also take over this part of the job for them.

Controlled temperature in farrowing houses will permit the moving of better-grade hogs to market in a little more than 100 (instead of 180) days after weaning, with a resultant lower life-loss of young pigs and less consumption of feed. The heat pump is already finding employment here.

Air conditioning, automatically controlled, will be standard practice in fruit and vegetable storage buildings. Electricity will provide the muscle power for handling the products in and out of storage, for cooling, washing, grading, and packing. Radiation equipment will be used in the larger potato storage plants to inhibit sprouting and thus allow longer periods of storage with less shrinkage and less loss of quality.

The greatest use of electricity in farm production today is in the pumping of water for irrigation. With the increasing need to conserve water, one of the greatest potential uses of electrical power may lie in the supplying of pressure for sprinkler irrigation. Tests have indicated that, for the same production, sprinkler application takes 16 per cent less water than surface application.

None of these uses for electricity on the farm are visionary; most are being employed somewhere on farms today. In toto, they present a bright picture of production for the farmer of the future, and they help to explain why automation—in the true sense of the word—may come at least as fast on the farm as in industry, and perhaps faster. And research and development are continuing to find ways to make electricity more useful and more beneficial; in this sense we can never have a completely electrified home or factory or farm.

For the farm home, we can predict all the appliances now being visualized in the laboratories of manufacturers. Farm families can legitimately claim consumer leadership in the acceptance and utilization of electric appliances; it is a significant fact that more electricity was used last year in farmers' homes than for all other farm operations. Only 20 or 30 years ago living conditions on most American farms were primitive, but many farm families today enjoy a higher standard of living—in terms of number of electric appliances, from which so much comfort and convenience is derived—than city families.

The warmth and cheer of the traditional old farm kitchen will not be lost, however, for the appliances will be designed in warm pretty colors and to fit together. Laundry chores will be reduced to absolute simplicity by a projected device for the complete treatment of soiled clothing through washing, drying, and processing to the final stage of clean folded clothes ready to wear.

The sink will combine in a single unit all the functions of food washing and preparation, ice supply, and garbage disposal. The refrigerator, on the other hand, may be available in each of the places it is needed: an ice supply at the sink, a cool drink and snack compartment in the family room, a fruit and vegetable storage unit near the preparation area, and a frozen-food storage unit next to the range.

The television screen will be on the wall, and an electronic recording tape that will hold both sound and picture will permit playbacks of favorite, or missed, programs.

The source of at least some of the electric power of the future will be atomic; other energy sources, solar or the fuel cell, may prove to be useful for special applications. But as far as we can see into the future, there is nothing to displace electricity as the most useful form of energy, or the electric motor as the most useful power package. We can thus expect electricity to continue its dual role of helping to provide both more goods and more leisure, with greater opportunities for physical, cultural, and spiritual enjoyment for the average family.

Charles G. Mortimer, chairman and chief executive of General Foods Corporation, has been active in the food industry since 1921. He was president of General Foods from April, 1954 until October, 1959, when he was elected chairman. He is also president of the Nutrition Foundation.

As one of the leading food processing companies in the country, General Foods' interest in foods extends from the farm to the table. The company has contributed to improvements in food processing and preservation—especially in the development of convenience foods—and has done extensive research in the field of nutrition.

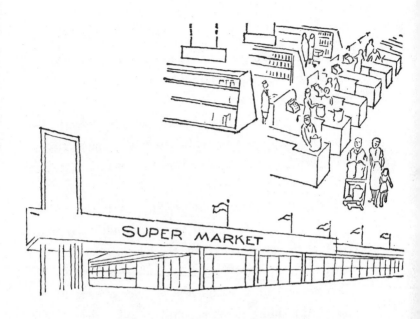

More and Better Food
for More People

Charles G. Mortimer

CONCERN with the nation's ability to meet the unprecedented challenge of feeding a 1975 population—which some estimates place as high as 245 million—may tend to overshadow some key facts.

This is not a population increase that will suddenly take place 15 years from now. Continuing growth in population is a characteristic of our history: the factors that could produce a population gain of as much as 65 million by 1975 are in motion right now and have been for many years. The size of increase varies with the times: the rate over any one period is affected by what has happened immediately before that period—war, perhaps, or the ups and down that punctuate the flow of our free economy.

Today we are not only feeding 40 million more Americans than we did in 1940—plus additional millions elsewhere throughout the world—but we are feeding them better than any people has been fed in all history. And, although the number of persons engaged in farming is some 2 million lower than it was in 1940 and the acreage devoted to crop production has similarly decreased, we have enormous crop surpluses.

To buy today's better-than-ever foods, Americans need work fewer hours than ever before. Unlike other lands, where an increasing population acts to create greater strain on the national economy, our country has actually benefited from the net increases in population that have continued to mark our history. More people—more consumers, more producing workers—has meant a greater contribution to the nation's overall economy.

Between 1940 and 1950, the net population increase in the United States was 19 million. By 1955, there were 14 million more people in the country. Thus the *rate* of net increase rose from an average of 1.9 million a year in one decade to 2.8 million a year in the next half decade. This has further risen to a 3 million rate at present. In other words, our population now increases by 8,000 persons a day, or 333 an hour, or we have over 5 additional mouths to feed every minute. With a population increase of 65 million by 1975, the average annual rate will increase over 40 percent, or 4.3 million a year. This means that, to the present net increase of 3 million a year, 1.3 million will be added. Instead of 8,000 a day, the increase will be almost 12,000; instead of 333 an hour, the gain will be almost 500; and every minute, instead of 5, there will be more than 8 additional mouths to feed.

A major factor in all future population estimates is that in the 1960–1970 decade some 33 million war babies will come of age. This is the largest single addition of new independent producers, wage earners, and consumers of any 10-year period in our history; as they marry and start new family units, they will have an enormous impact on America's economy and future population status. This group, even more than preceding generations, will have the traditional American urge to "trade up," in food, automobiles, television sets, furniture, and other consumer goods. And, in the same decade, there will be upwards of 17 million people over 65—more than at any previous period in our history. With lengthened life expectancy they, too, will continue to strive toward a better life.

Year after year, more people have been able to avail themselves of a great variety of convenience foods, goods, and services that, not too many years before, were to them either entirely unknown or unattainable luxuries. Lower unit costs, attributable to a higher volume of production, have brought these products within reach of a greater number of people. At the same time, the steadily improving quality of these products has resulted in a constantly better flow of values that attract an ever-increasing number of consumers.

The higher productivity and advances in technology that continue to accompany increasing population in the United States can reasonably be expected to stimulate still greater progress, thanks to our free-enterprise system. What has happened in recent years affords a measure of the insistence of Americans on having food with built-in convenience and quality, together with appealing taste and satisfying flavor. For the last quarter century, Americans have spent between 22 and 28 per cent of their disposable income on food. Before World War II, it was some 23 per cent. If we were willing today to buy the same food as before World War II, we could do so for about 16 per cent of current disposable income, even at today's higher postwar prices. But today we spend about 25 per cent of disposable income for foods; in other words, we are eating better.

All indications are that disposable income will continue to rise and that with rising income the trend away from such tedious chores as chicken plucking, fish cleaning, spinach desanding, potato peeling, and orange squeezing will be accelerated. There will be an increasing demand for the high-quality trouble-free time-saving convenience foods that fit so well into modern living.

The mobility of the population and its shifts to urban living that have characterized postwar America have challenged the entire lifeline of our nation from farm furrow to checkout counter. And the challenge, which involves growers, processors, shippers, wholesalers, and chain and independent distributors, transcends the mere logistics of feeding an ever-greater number of people.

The big challenge is to provide better-balanced meals that will protect and enhance the health of a people increasingly alert to the benefits of proper nutrition. Food technologists and the medical profession are concerned with building a complete hunger satisfaction into foods that provide, at the same time, good-quality proteins and vitamin and mineral balance. The combined satisfaction of a full meal and one that supplies all of the necessary nutrients is the goal. The first, of course, is the satisfaction of hunger that comes when the stomach is full; the second, the well-being that comes when all our metabolic needs are met. The ultimate aim is to develop tasty convenience foods that satisfy both our hunger and our nutrient needs, but at a lower caloric level. We cater to a society that will probably be even more calorie-conscious than it is today, one in which foods will be used to prevent rather than combat obesity and disease. Foods will be used constructively and purposefully as chemical building blocks for man's growth, and as fuel for more efficient energizing of nature's most complex machine. And these foods will taste good, too.

A sufficient awareness of the importance of food has already been created and enough far-ranging research has been initiated to indicate that the higher population of the future will be even better fed than we are today. Science, which already has given us a multitude of new foods and combinations of foods with which to cater to the needs, tastes, and convenience of the consumer, will provide us with the additional nutrition that an increasingly more knowledgeable population will demand. Just as food growers have stretched the productive capacity of each acre of land, so food processors will expand the nutritional value of each meal consumed.

Past accomplishments attest the ability of the food industry to meet the challenges of sharp increases in population. New and better ways of processing, handling, and distributing food have more than kept pace with the population increase following World War II, and adjustments have been made swiftly as America's mobility increased and the unprecedented shift to urban living soared. With the help of automation, a constant stream of products required by the American kind of living has been provided. Foods in processing plants are prepared, packaged, and made ready for shipment and distribution via warehouses so located as to meet best the needs of heavily populated metropolitan centers.

New events are constantly occurring in the food industry. For example, terms that not long ago were only familiar to technologists are now being incorporated into the vocabularies of executives in production, marketing, and other areas. Some of these terms —irradiation, antibiotics, ultrasonics, and dehydro-freezing—have something to do with food preservation, an area which in the next few years is likely to feel an enormous impact from change.

Food irradiation is now under extensive study by government, by private industry, by a combination of these two important elements in our society, and by other scientists in the laboratories of many of our colleges and universities. From such studies, we know that foods which have been sterilized by being placed in a field of ionizing radiation will, with proper packaging, remain sterile for a considerable length of time. The process has already been demonstrated with meat, milk, fruit, vegetables, and other foods. And research in this field is continuing. As experience in the early days of frozen foods showed, even though bacterial activity is halted, chemical and enzymatic reactions continue to take place. Irradiation also affects to some extent the taste and texture of foods. In the future quick freezing—which preserves flavor and texture— will probably be combined with irradiation to increase the cabinet life of some foods. Similarly, a combination of antibiotics and irradiation seems to offer promise for an increased storage life of many foods. These combinations and other developments may even lead us to the day when the crops of surplus years can be stored relatively inexpensively for use in lean years.

Encouraging to researchers are some of the findings by the Surgeon General's office and the Quartermaster Corps of the United States Army, whose scientists are studying the effects of irradiation on public health. It has already been established that foods sterilized by this process do not become radioactive, just as a human being does not become radioactive after a chest X ray. When approved methods are used, this process in no way endangers health.

The use of antibiotics in the preservation of food gained official recognition as far back as 1945. Since the particular antibiotics used for this purpose are sensitive to heat, they are completely destroyed in the cooking. Today the Food and Drug Administration permits their use in preserving dressed poultry, and their use may well be extended to the preservation of fish and meat. They are also being used with some success in surface treatment for harvested fruits and vegetables to prevent spoilage during shipment and in stores.

The sterilization of food by the dehydro-freezing method is already well advanced. This process consists in first dehydrating (removing part of the water) and then quick-freezing foods. To avoid undesirable changes, drying is accomplished with the least possible heat, which lessens considerably the danger of cellular damage during freezing. The resulting product is lighter in weight and smaller in bulk than the original and has the advantages of savings in freight costs and storage shelf space. Experiments in the use of this process with fruits, vegetables, and some other foods have already advanced to the market-test stage.

Ultrasonics (high-frequency inaudible sound waves) have been used by scientists to sterilize food by vibration; the life is literally shaken out of the bacteria that produce decay. These waves have been used to produce a number of chemical and physical changes in food, but so far, only the surface possibilities have been explored.

Early results have been promising in the fields of sterilization, homogenization, extraction, and dehydration. Although no practical application has been found up to now, food technologists hope to produce practical results that will be important to the homemaker of tomorrow. Irradiation, antibiotics, dehydro-freezing, and ultrasonics represent new methods of food preservation, some of which will undoubtedly help solve the problem of feeding our increasing millions. They are, at the moment, those that hold the most promise, but food scientists in government, industry, and university laboratories will doubtless, as time goes on, come up with even better methods of food preservation.

The final judge in these areas will be the consumer or, in other words, the homemaker. She is the boss. She has high standards of quality, taste, nutrition, and convenience, and she wants all four every time. She wants to save time, and she wants foods that can be conveniently prepared, that take the drudgery and the gamble out of cooking. She wants to maintain balanced diets for her family, including protective foods. More and more she relies on the processor for balance in the diets of all members of her family, and the nutritive qualities of various foods are being increasingly stressed by the processors who enjoy her confidence. To the homemaker, who is concerned with the health and nourishment of her family, meal planning and preparation is not simply a responsibility, but a major creative outlet. Her kitchen is the ultimate proving ground for the food developed by the scientists and will continue to be as important as their laboratories in bringing about changes in the eating habits of the future.

But good nutrition must not be attained at the expense of good flavor. The homemaker wants food products and recipes for dishes that she not only can serve easily but with a feeling that she is taking proper care of her family; she wants to satisfy their tastes as well as their basic needs.

Will the homemaker's habits in the matter of foods keep pace with the changes that will undoubtedly occur in the food-processing industry? Will she, for example, buy foods preserved by new methods, if they fulfill their promise? The record shows that, when she finds that they suit her requirements, she will. There may be some reluctance at first, just as back in the early 1930's, when quick-frozen foods were first marketed. Homemakers first associated quick-frozen foods with the "cold storage" foods whose reputation was poor. It required extensive educational advertising over a number of years to convince homemakers that what was then a revolutionary new method of food preservation brought prepared, ready-to-cook garden-fresh fruits, vegetables, and other foods to their kitchens— with quality and taste intact—at all seasons. So it will be with the new food products as they come from laboratories and pilot plants. The homemakers of the new generation start where their mothers left off, and each succeeding generation is prone to accept new things more quickly and easily.

In addition to learning more about the preservation of foods, processors are learning more and more about how to control and eliminate waste and spoilage. In speeding up operations to meet the ultimate demands of a growing population, their work on the development of synthetic foods is also being stepped up. And researchers will keep trying to make the sea, as well as the soil, give up secrets that will make possible the feeding—and better feeding, at that—of more and more people and, it is hoped, at lower and lower relative costs.

Just as the homemaker is at the heart of progress in the processing of foods, she is also the one who must be satisfied with the changes that seem bound to occur in the great supermarkets where tomorrow's foods will be sold. Already marvels of efficiency, these markets are continually experimenting with ways and means to provide still greater efficiencies. When the manager of a supermarket plans his weekly order in 1975—and perhaps even a decade before that—he will quite probably not work from an order pad. Instead, as he walks through the store he will radio his order directly to an electronic order-receiving machine at a central warehouse. There, in a few seconds, his order will be received, checked against merchandise in stock, and routed to the order assembly areas—all automatically. When the merchandise arrives at the store, it will enter a moving-belt system. Prices will be placed on packages automatically, and the packages will move directly to the shelves. Preset electronic controls will automatically load each shelf with its predetermined number of packages, with each taking its preset facing and shelf position. At that all-important point, the check-out counter, things will be improved too and speeded up. All the buyer will have to do is place his packages on the counter with the prices facing up. The check-out marvel will do the rest; it will automatically total the order from the prices stamped on the packages and pack and send the completed order out of the store to the parking lot pick-up point.

What does all of this add up to? In an age of rapid growth, on the basis of experiments already under way or on the drawing boards, we can predict some of the changes in the food industry which, in only a few years, may be well advanced. Quantitatively, we can feed the expanded population of 1975; technical advances will see to this. The principal challenge lies not only in feeding more people but in feeding them better, in developing better nutrition and better-balanced diets while catering to higher levels of taste and ensuring greater ease and convenience in the production of those foods that enable people to enjoy fuller and longer lives.

To achieve these goals, we will need to have available the skill of better-educated and better-trained people in all walks of life. We will need the combined competence of farmers, scientists, processors, transporters, and distributors. Most of all, we will need to understand the consumer's requirements as they are upgraded in a society which, hopefully, will place ever-greater emphasis on quality. Knowing the higher levels of tastes of the people—even anticipating them—is a growing responsibility in food processing and marketing. Science and its developments will play a big role in our future, but in the final analysis it is the people, and what they want, that are most important.

Charles B. Shuman is a livestock, grain, and grassland farmer. He lives on and participates in the operation of his home farm near Sullivan, Ill., which has been in the Shuman family since 1853. He was graduated from the University of Illinois in 1928, and in 1929 earned his master's degree in agronomy at the same institution.

Mr. Shuman has served as president of the Moultrie County Farm Bureau and the Illinois Agricultural Association. Since 1954, he has been president of the American Farm Bureau Federation, an organization of 1,600,000 farm families.

The Man on the Farm

Charles B. Shuman

ALARMISTS are often heard to cry that the family farm is about to disappear from the American scene, that corporate farming is about to take over the production of food and fiber. But a realistic look at the farms of the United States shows that these alarmists, perhaps with design, are choosing to ignore a true and wholesome development in agriculture: family farms are getting bigger and stronger.

I see no threat to the family farm in this country as long as food and fiber are produced by cultivating the land and raising domestic animals. As long as food comes from the soil and not from chemical or other processes that are adaptable to factory use, the family unit will be a tough competitor for a large-scale corporate enterprise. Were this not so, the corporate system would have taken over long ago.

What exactly is the family farm? It is a production unit, controlled and operated by the farmer and his family. At times the family farm uses outside hired help; more often it does not. An enterprise does not cease to be a family farm merely because it grows to the point where the operator's family must hire more labor than it can provide from its own resources. What is important is that the individual farm family has a close identity with the ownership, operation, and control of its own business, in contrast to the position of the hired manager who works for absentee owners.

As to the ability of the American family farm to increase its efficiency, the production record to date, itself gives the best evidence. In 1940, the labor of a farm worker supplied 11 people with food and fiber. Today, a single farm worker supplies the needs of 26 people. Today, with 30 per cent less farm employment and 43 million more people than in 1940, our family farms are supplying the nation with more nourishment and more raw material per capita than ever before. And we have by no means exhausted our ability to meet the expanding needs of a growing population for farm-produced food and fiber.

There are some who say that agriculture has gone through a great technological revolution; but are we not, in fact, only on the threshold of that revolution? Since many of the more spectacular advances in agricultural technology are of fairly recent origin, it is hardly likely that possibilities of this nature are exhausted. The probability is that the scientific agricultural technology, of which we all are so proud, is still in its infancy. Constantly, new developments are making it possible for the farmer to spread his labor over more acres and a larger number of animals or birds.

These developments will also have a profound economic impact. The net income of those farm families who are able and willing to adjust to the new conditions will be raised. At the same time, many rural people will be released to do other jobs in industry and business, in the arts, sciences, and professions. Urban people will feel the impact of new and expanded markets for their goods and services, while a greater variety of better quality food and fiber products is made available to them by this new-day agriculture.

Farming is a business—it is highly competitive. Farmers compete not only with each other but also with the producers of synthetics, chemicals, vitamin pills, and foreign food and fiber. The family farm will remain the dominant unit in American agriculture if goverment policies are directed toward encouraging farmers to adjust to meet competition rather than toward preventing change.

Government has a role to play in agriculture. I am convinced that it is possible for farmers to earn and receive a high per family real income, provided we can define the proper activities of government in such basic areas of concern to agriculture as research, education, economics, and inflation.

The need for research is obvious. New problems continue to arise. Many doors remain locked. Only a very material increase in the level of agricultural research and communications will enable farmers to keep pace with the rapidly changing competitive economy in which we live. Synthetic substitutes could replace many farm products in consumer markets if we fail to keep our products competitive in price and quality. Two million small, independent farm units cannot carry on an adequate program of fundamental research.

Furthermore, the public has a definite interest in the basic research which must be carried on if we are to produce an adequate food supply for our expanding population. Yes, government support for research can be justified on these grounds and it also helps farmers make the necessary changes to meet competitive conditions.

The family farm has proven to be the most efficient unit for utilizing this new knowledge. Naturally, the size of the farm operation must continue to expand and the farm operator's ability must be such that he can put this new knowledge to the most efficient and effective use.

Education, therefore, is of great importance in agriculture. In order to be maintained, an educational system, controlled and supported by the smallest government unit able to meet the necessary standards, must be geared to solving the problems facing the people of an immediate area. New general basic information must be made available to local areas for the solution of local problems. Education provides the farmer with the opportunity to absorb this new knowledge, which he needs for the growth and expansion of his operation. It increases his ability to handle larger operations by providing him with answers to his production and marketing problems. It enables him to understand better the forces constantly at work to change his future.

Young people from the farm should be encouraged to go as far with their formal education as their resources and abilities will permit, for today's business-type agriculture demands better generally informed and better-trained operators. College-trained men and women can find satisfying and challenging opportunities on our modern productive farms, and we shall need increasing numbers of college-trained people to handle the growing family enterprises and to utilize the complicated techniques of the future.

There are many areas of agricultural research other than those concerned with increased yields. The farm family is just as vitally affected by research into new uses for farm products, new crops, marketing, human nutrition, and product modification. Marketing furnishes a good example of an area that needs much study.

Farmers long have been unhappy with the marketing system for agricultural products. We have complained about the wide spread between prices paid by consumers and receipts of farmers for a commodity. Ours is one of the few businesses that delivers its product to market with little or no advance arrangements on either the quantity that is to be delivered or the price that is to be paid. Many attempts have been made to improve our marketing efficiency and to increase our bargaining power. Although marketing cooperatives, bargaining associations, marketing agreements, and other devices have been used to some advantage, basic problems still persist.

Perhaps much of our marketing difficulty stems from the traditional pattern of farm operation—volume production of bulk commodities with little concern for consumer preference: fat hogs, overweight steers, mixed wheat, ungraded eggs, high-moisture grain, and poor-quality fruits and vegetables. This system worked fairly well in the days of the general store with its cracker barrel and low-priced bulk food. Today, the food industry, from the farm to the supermarket, is highly competitive, and our customers are more particular. The modern food market carries several thousand items. If the fresh vegetables are of low quality, the housewife turns to canned or frozen products. If the pork is overfat, she chooses other meat.

The women of America are specification buyers. The retailer passes these customer specifications on to the processor, and he in turn must try to obtain the desired type of product from farmers. Specification buying explains much of the current increase in contractual marketing and the evolution of vertical integration in agriculture. As with anything new, some farmers are for and others are against contractual marketing. Change, nevertheless, is inevitable and if contractual marketing fulfills an economic need, it will continue to increase whether we like it or not.

Contracts for production of goods to meet certain specifications have long been used by business and industry to reduce risk. Contracts have been used to advantage by farmers who produce canning crops, sugar beets, and other commodities. Farmers need a device to reduce marketing risks and uncertainties.

We would like to reduce the number of middlemen required to handle, sort, and recondition our products. Before starting the costly process of producing a crop, we should know something of the desired quality, quantity, and price of the finished product. Contractual marketing may be a step toward these desired results. In any event, the contract is a tool that farmers may be able to use as they organize to improve their bargaining and marketing ability.

Change, like knowledge, is essential and cumulative. Just how fast changes take place depends on many things, including the knowledge available to build new techniques. As these changes and related knowledge accumulate, avenues must be kept open for a free flow of resources among all segments of the economy.

Markets for production supplies and for farm products must remain in private hands so that changing demands for different types of supplies and products will be reflected through market prices. Unless markets are free, production patterns will be frozen, resources will be unwisely used, and huge stocks of unwanted goods may accumulate. Such developments burden consumers by raising prices and by preventing the market from making available the goods that are wanted. Here, again, the proper role of government is in creating a favorable climate for the effective operation of the free market price system.

A major problem facing farmers today is that national agricultural legislation to fix prices and control production has actually stimulated production without regard for market needs. Any program which expands

farm production in the absence of a comparable increase in effective market demand is generally contrary
to the best interests of producers and the economy.
Likewise, programs which encourage inefficient production render a disservice to agriculture by contribut-
ing to surplus accumulation, increasing average production costs and limiting output per man. There is a
proper place for government price supports to encourage orderly marketing and prevent drastic seasonal
price declines. However, experience has clearly shown
that programs to fix prices and control production do
not ensure satisfactory farm income. In fact, much of
the recent decline in farm prices is due to the loss of
markets and surplus accumulation which result from
unsuccessful efforts of the government to price and
control certain crops. We must move as rapidly as possible away from government activity of this kind—it has
not worked and it hinders the individual farmer's efforts
to adjust to meet changed conditions.

Private ownership of capital resources and the ability
of farmers to accumulate capital also are both necessary
if farming in the future is to meet with success. Capital
resources include money, long- and short-term credit
facilities, and property such as land, power facilities,
and irrigation networks. Large capital investments are

required by modern agriculture, and the requirements increase with technological advances.

Currently, the average investment per worker on the farm is more than that of the worker in almost any other industry, and this investment will, relatively speaking, continue to increase. Without this high capital investment, the farmer would be condemned to a life of hard, back-breaking hand labor, and he would find it very difficult to feed the growing population of America at current dietary levels.

Credit facilities both for beginning farmers and those who wish to expand the size of their farm business must, therefore, be improved. The individual farmer's ability to utilize his resources and build for himself a profitable livelihood from agriculture is limited by his supply of capital and credit. A constantly improving standard of living in agriculture is dependent upon the ability of farmers to accumulate capital and to own property.

Inflation is a barrier to accumulation of capital necessary for modern agriculture. The equally unsatisfactory counterpart is, of course, serious deflation and depression. Inflation destroys the incentive to save and encourages overexpansion in terms of current consumption, since the value of money is impaired by declines in its purchasing power. Serious economic downturns increase capital consumption and reduce investment possibilities, bringing economic growth and improvement of living standards to a standstill.

National monetary and fiscal policy should be so operated as to avoid the economic ills of both inflation and serious deflation or depression. Monetary and fiscal policy changes should benefit the entire national economy; they must not be used piecemeal to favor some groups over others.

Farmers are interested in ample money and credit at reasonable costs and in lower tax burdens; but they are also interested in checking inflationary pressures and avoiding depressions. Farmers, like all other Americans, have much to gain by policies that will bring reductions in government spending and provide adequate checks and balances for both inflationary and deflationary pressures.

As agriculture becomes more and more specialized and dependent upon the nonfarm sectors of the economy, the proper functioning of the entire economic system takes on added importance. Agriculture is no longer a simple agrarian occupation; it is not merely a way of life; it is a business, and for its successful operation those who are engaged in it need to have an ever greater understanding of the nonagricultural forces at work in the economy. As the size of the individual family farming operation continues to grow, farmers will use more nonagricultural goods and services; and as the number of persons engaged in these agricultural operations declines proportionately, the farm organizations will become more and more important as the voice of the farmer.

The economic forces of the nation have been influenced heavily by the political forces of government. But economic forces are like laws of nature: they operate eventually, regardless of the efforts of people to stop them. To stifle the operation of economic forces is to stifle the operation of individuals. Many governments have tried to halt economic forces, and the people have suffered or they have revolted and the governments have fallen by the wayside of history.

The United States was the first country in history to erect an economic and political system whereby the problems of the people were to be solved by the people themselves. This system, based on free individual enterprise, has given us a country with 7 per cent of the world's population living on 6 per cent of the world's land area and 44 per cent of all the wealth that has been amassed in the world. Freedom of the individual to do as he chooses, within a set of defined rules, has been the driving force that has made America the strongest, richest, and freest country in the history of civilization.

The function of government, as established in the Declaration of Independence and the Constitution, is to act as a referee in the economic system in the enforcement of the rules of competition and fair play. But it seems that some groups in the economy are now trying to create an entirely different function for government in the belief that the government should attempt to insulate the individual from the pressures of change in an industrial nation.

Since sharp and violent economic fluctuations do cause considerable social as well as individual damage, the stabilizing actions of government have, in some areas, contributed to our growth and betterment. But when the government goes beyond attempts to cushion adjustments and to stabilize the economy, society as a whole is hurt more than it is helped.

When the government maintains people in a given status through doles and patronage, the dignity of the individual and his incentives, which are the foundation of the economy, are destroyed. In cushioning adjustments, the government should do just that and no more. Adjustments must take place, but when they do, it is crueler to maintain people in a given status of low opportunity than to encourage them to move to new areas of endeavor.

The primary requirement for a successful agriculture in the future is that the economic and political systems remain free to make adjustments. The farmer's freedom to expand and to change in accordance with his ability and the resources available to him must not be hindered either by government policy or the restrictive practices of nongovernment groups. Resources, both human and material, must be permitted to flow where they can best be used. Markets must be allowed to function freely so that farmers can know and meet the demands of consumers.

If these requirements are met and the farmer has the assurance that he can enjoy these freedoms, there is no question that he will be able to supply ample food for America's future.